Project Control Methods and Best Practices

Project Control Methods and Best Practices

Achieving Project Success

Yakubu Olawale

BEP

BUSINESS EXPERT PRESS

Leader in applied, concise business books

Project Control Methods and Best Practices: Achieving Project Success

First published in 2022 by
Business Expert Press, LLC
222 East 46th Street, New York, NY 10017
www.businessexpertpress.com

ISBN-13: 978-1-63742-299-1 (paperback)
ISBN-13: 978-1-63742-300-4 (e-book)

Business Expert Press Portfolio and Project Management Collection

First edition: 2022

10 9 8 7 6 5 4 3 2 1

To my wife Tokunbo with love, and my children, Nancy, Nathan, and William, thanks for your support.

And to the memory of my loving mother, Victoria Toyin Yakubu, 1955–2022, who instilled in me the penchant for scholarly excellence, words can't describe the vacuum you've left in our hearts.

Description

If you want to know how to reduce financial wastage and cost overrun on projects and the applied best practices to enable project success, then this book is for you.

This book reveals the many challenges of project control in practice and then provides practical good practices to overcome them. This is done by presenting a robust research-informed project control framework that includes several good practices to mitigate project control inhibitors and enhance the entire project control process. The core project control techniques and methods in practice and how to design an enabling environment for effective project control are also explained.

The aim of this book is to expose the readers to several good practices which they can then apply confidently to enhance the success of their projects.

Keywords

project control; project success; project management; cost management; time management; schedule management; PCIM

Contents

Testimonials xi

Abbreviations and Acronyms xiii

Chapter 1   Introduction 1

**Part 1   Achieving Effective Project Controls Using the
PCIM Project Control Methodology 19**

Chapter 2   Fundamental Concepts of Project Control 21

Chapter 3   Project Control in Practice and Prevention of
Challenges to Effective Project Control 35

Chapter 4   Using the Project Control Inhibitors Management
(PCIM) Methodology to Improve Project Control
in Practice 59

Chapter 5   Good Practices to Mitigate the Foremost Project
Cost and Time Control Inhibitors 75

Chapter 6   Good Practices for the Cyclic Project Control
Steps: Planning, Monitoring, Reporting, and
Analyzing 101

**Part 2   Classical Techniques Used During
Project Control 119**

Chapter 7   Classical Project Time Control Techniques 121

Chapter 8   Classical Project Cost Control Techniques 145

Chapter 9   Project Scope Management 165

Chapter 10   Risk Management 175

Chapter 11   Overview of Supplier Performance Management,
Business Case, and Benefits Management Processes 191

Chapter 12   The Ingredients of an Effective Project Control
Environment 203

References 209

About the Author 213

Index 215

Testimonials

"Projects are so much part of business today, yet we struggle with the control aspect more than ever. The beauty of this book is the applied approach that encourages the reader to transfer the ideas into their practice in order to realise greater success. The clarity and accessibility of the ideas and writing suggest it should be on the bookshelf of anyone engaged in project management practice or study."—**Professor Robin Clark, Dean of WMG, University of Warwick, UK**

"The publication of this book is timely. Delivering successful projects has never been more important in terms of economic and wider societal wellbeing. This book provides many excellent insights into the critical success factors. It is based on Dr Olawale's unique blend of extensive practical project management experience in a variety of settings and the academic rigour that his strong research background brings."—**Professor Edward Sweeney, Edinburgh Business School, Heriot Watt University, UK**

Abbreviations and Acronyms

3-D	three-dimensional
4-D	four-dimensional
5-D	five-dimensional
AC	actual cost
ACWP	actual cost of work performed
ADM	arrow diagram method
APM	Association for Project Management
BCWP	budgeted cost of work performed
BCWS	budgeted cost of work scheduled
BoK	Body of Knowledge
CBS	cost breakdown structure
COVID-19	coronavirus disease 2019
CPI	cost performance index
CPM	critical path method
CV	cost variance
CVR	cost value reconciliation
DfT	Department for Transport
EAC	estimate at completion
ESG	environment, social, and governance
EV	earned value
EVA	earned value analysis
EVM	earned value management
FS	finish-to-start
GERT	graphical evaluation and review technique
IAS	Internal Accounting Standards
ICE	Institution of Civil Engineers
IChemE	Institution of Chemical Engineers
IFRS	International Financial Reporting Standards
IT	information technology

JCT	Joint Contracts Tribunal
KPI	key performance indicator
LOB	line of balance
M&E	mechanical and electrical
MS Project	Microsoft Project
NHS	The UK National Health Service
PBS	product breakdown structure
PCAS	project cost accounting system
PCID	project control implementation document
PCIM	project control inhibitors management
PCP	project control plan
PDM	precedence diagram method
PEP	project execution plan
PERT	performance evaluation and review technique
PEST	political, economic, social, technological
PESTLE	political, economic, social, technological, legal, environmental
PhD	doctor of philosophy
PIs	performance indicators
PMI	Project Management Institute
PV	planned value
QCRA	quantitative cost risk analysis
QS	quantity surveyor
QSRA	quantitative schedule risk analysis
R&D	research and development
ROI	return on investment
SAC	schedule at completion
SPI	schedule performance index
SPORT	social, political, organizational, regulatory, technological
SV	schedule variance
TfL	Transport for London
UNESCO	United Nations Educational, Scientific, and Cultural Organization
VAC	variance at completion
WBS	work breakdown structure

CHAPTER 1

Introduction

Introduction to Project Control

Projects help organizations achieve their goals and strategic objectives. For example, 95 percent of government policies in the UK are delivered through major projects (National Audit Office 2013). Put simply, business outcomes are affected by the success of projects. Therefore, project-focused practice is common for many organizations in different industrial sectors, from an oil company developing an exploration site, to an investment bank installing a new IT system; from a technology company developing and launching a new type of gadget, to the government of a country constructing a new high-speed rail infrastructure. One of the distinguishing features of projects is that they are normally required to be completed within specified timeframe, scope, and an allocated cost budget. However, many projects are not delivered successfully, impacting negatively on organizational earnings and profitability. Control is the recognized mechanism to prevent project failure and keep a project on track. Even though the importance of project control during the implementation of projects is obvious, research indicates that many projects still fail from a cost and time performance perspective.

The classic research by Flyvbjerg, Holm, and Buhl (2003) across 20 countries and five continents, showed that nine out of every ten projects encounter cost overrun, indicating this as a global phenomenon. Research by the project management institute (PMI) (2020) revealed that organizations globally wasted an average of $114 million for every $1 billion spent on projects due to poor project performance. This problem is common across various industries in the economy, for example, construction industry: $127 million wasted for every $1 billion spent; energy industry: $113 million wasted for every $1 billion spent; government: $97 million wasted for every $1 billion spent; health care industry: $113 wasted for every $1 billion spent. High-profile examples of projects with such financial wastage include:

- Berlin's New Brandenburg Airport, which exceeded budget by 41 percent and time by 9 years (O'Neil 2019);
- Denver International Airport: 194 percent over budget and 1.3 years late (Jergeas and Ruwanpura 2010);
- Scottish Parliament: £400 million over budget and 3 years late (Flyvbjerg 2017; O'Neil 2019);
- Crossrail: £4 billion over budget and 3.5 years late (Reuters 2022).

So, what's the answer to avoid situations like the above? Poor performance and financial waste in projects can be avoided by setting up a well-designed and intelligent project control process, supported by good practices and the right culture that will enable projects to be delivered more successfully. Research by Pollack and Adler (2016) showed that organizations with effective project management skills have a 75.5 percent chance of increase in profitability compared with organizations without them. But if project controls are not carried out consistently and designed intelligently, they won't be effective. Furthermore, control is one of the major tools of project management. It has been stated by the Association for Project Management (APM) (2015) that "effective project management requires effective control." Project control involves measuring progress constantly, evaluating plans, and taking corrective actions when required. In essence, project control is the application of processes to measure project performance against the project plan, to enable variances, to be identified and corrected, so that project objectives are achieved (APM 2010) including keeping projects on track and within budget. But this is easier said than done. Establishing and following effective project control is a multifaceted, sometimes complex process, which is often not done consistently within organizations.

Traditionally, as argued by Sanchez, Terlizzi, and Moraes (2017), the inherent task of successful project management has been to deliver the outputs of the project on time, within the budget, and to the required scope. Which has led these three areas (cost, time, and scope) to stand out when it comes to control. Time control, also often referred to as schedule control, is the aspect of project management that involves the management of the time spent and progress made on project tasks and activities with the aim of completing the project on time. Cost control involves the management and technical procedures used to manage the delivery of a project within the planned budget, whereas scope control is the process of managing the project's outputs and changes to the outputs to enable delivery of what was agreed.

Effective project control helps save costs and improve return on investment. When deployed consistently using good practices, project control can increase management's visibility of the financial performance of the projects to allow for the development of mitigation plans to improve the performance of poor performing projects. Effective project control also makes it easier to predict how long projects will take and how much they'll cost, reduce costs, improve company margins, and provide organizations with a competitive advantage over organizations with less mature project control capabilities.

Introduction to the Process of Project Control

The objectives of a project such as delivery at the required time, scope, and budget will be difficult to achieve unless the project is controlled. This is because delivery of projects does not always go perfectly to plan, which reflects the popular military saying attributed to the Prussian military leader of the 19th century, Helmuth von Moltke, that no plan survives contact with the enemy. Therefore, projects require a process for monitoring and managing in such a way that deviations from plan are detected and corrected timely. In practice, project control is an iterative process that is usually achieved in three phases: setting performance standards, comparing actual performance with these standards, and then taking necessary corrective actions. In a project environment, project control normally involves three operating modes: (1) measuring, which is determining progress by formal and informal reporting; (2) evaluating, which is determining the cause of deviations from the plan; (3) correcting, which is taking actions to put right any deviation from the plan. In essence, controlling the project involves the process of managing the many problems that arise during project execution to maintain the plan. The process of project control at its simplest form is depicted in Figure 1.1.

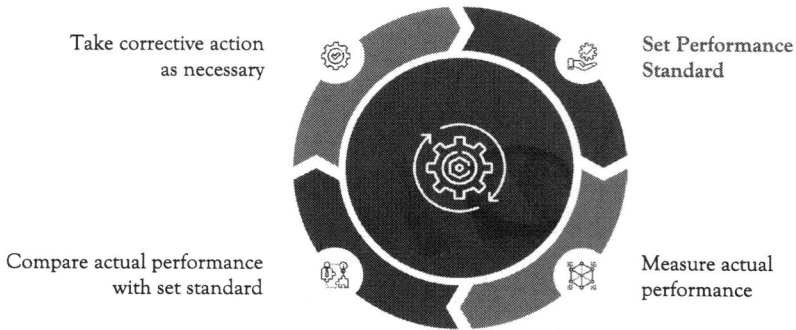

Figure 1.1 The basic process of project control

The key components of the process involve setting performance standards, performance measurement, comparison against the set standard, and corrective action. These are briefly explained below. However, a more detailed explanation is provided in Chapter 2 and referred to all through this book.

- *Setting project performance standards*: Targets are set for each project activity in terms of time, cost, quality, and so on. The plan for the project is used to set these standards, which then serve as the standards that are used to control the project.
- *Performance measurement*: This involves the measurement of the actual performance of each project activity as the project progresses to get feedback on how each activity is being performed and the performance of the whole project.
- *Comparison against the set performance standard*: During this process, the result of the actual performance measured is compared with the project standards set in the plan to determine deviation for each activity. This process also involves the analysis of the causes and prevalence of the deviations.
- *Take corrective actions*: If comparison and analysis indicate that the activities are deviating from the plan, corrective actions are then taken to improve the situation so that the activities can be brought back in line with the project plan. This part of the process is the crux of project control as it seeks to resolve any identified problem to get the project back on track.

Reasons for Embarking on Project Control in Practice

The main reason for the utilization of project control cannot be more obvious—it is to prevent cost overrun and delay (time overrun) of projects. Other reasons project management practitioners utilize project controls include:

- To ensure that the project progresses in an orderly manner;
- To enable efficient use of resources;
- To provide and/or obtain information and knowledge of the status of the project;
- Good management practice and part of a company's quality procedure;
- To provide more value to the client leading to client's satisfaction and repeat business.

The above reasons for embarking on project control in addition to the need to prevent project cost and time overrun are all geared at achieving the ultimate objective of the execution phase of a project, that is, to enable successful project performance. The performance of a project is normally measured in terms of one or more project objectives agreed at project inception. It is important to note that despite many objectives that a project may be subject to, the classical project performance objectives remain completing the project on time, to the required scope, and within budget. This is often referred to as the "iron triangle" or "triple constraint" (this is explained further in Chapter 2). It is therefore imperative to control these objectives during project delivery so that they are always in congruence with the plan to enable project delivery success.

When Has a Project Performed Successfully?

Traditionally, a project is considered successful if it is delivered on time, at the stated cost and quality/scope, and provides the client with a high level of satisfaction. Therefore, project success performance has usually been measured using factors related to budget, quality, and schedule (time) performance. For example, in measuring cost and time performance, two parameters are often used: cost growth and time growth. Cost growth is a measure of performance of cost control, that is, the final project cost divided by the initial project cost. While time growth is a measure of the performance of the project time plan, that is, the final project duration divided by initial project duration.

Despite a consensus that cost, time, and scope (including quality) are the key success criteria for projects, many commentators have argued that other factors should be considered in addition to them. For example, Davis (2014) stated that project success should also be viewed in relation to the perception of the project's stakeholders. Therefore, customer satisfaction is now often considered as a key project success criterion as Anantatmula and Rad (2018) have observed. Furthermore, the socioeconomic impact of projects has also broadened the project success metrics as stated by Zaman, Florez-Perez, Khwaja, Abbasi, and Qureshi (2021).

It is now perfectly acceptable, as Camilleri (2016) argued, to assert that success is subjective and varies according to the assessor and thus requires a more comprehensive set of criteria to encompass various views and interests (see Figure 1.2). Therefore, a distinction between project management success and project success is also often made. With the argument being that project management success is measured against the traditional success criteria of time, cost, and quality/scope while project success tends to be measured at a more strategic level by comparing the outcome to the overall project objectives.

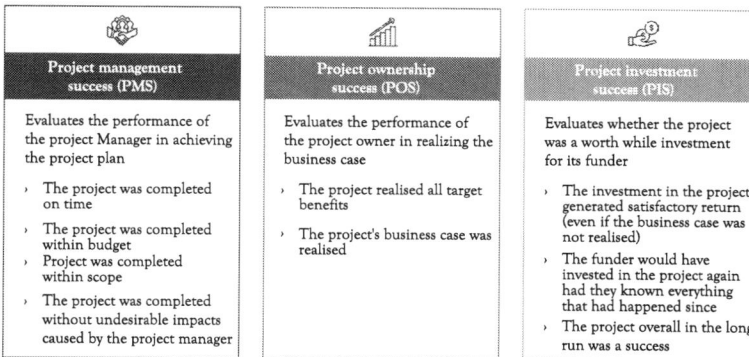

Project management success (PMS)	Project ownership success (POS)	Project investment success (PIS)
Evaluates the performance of the project Manager in achieving the project plan	Evaluates the performance of the project owner in realizing the business case	Evaluates whether the project was a worth while investment for its funder
› The project was completed on time › The project was completed within budget › Project was completed within scope › The project was completed without undesirable impacts caused by the project manager	› The project realised all target benefits › The project's business case was realised	› The investment in the project generated satisfactory return (even if the business case was not realised) › The funder would have invested in the project again had they known everything that had happened since › The project overall in the long run was a success

Figure 1.2 Example of a multistakeholder view of project success

Source: Zwikael and Meridith, 2021

For instance, Lock (2013) pointed out the three objectives of time, cost, and quality might be mostly related to the interests of the project manager, project team, and contracting parties delivering the work; however, other stakeholders might be more concerned in other success measures such as delivering business value, operational benefits, customer satisfaction, strategic impact, and so on. The Sydney Opera House is an example that is commonly used to prove that the triple constraints of time, cost, and quality do not epitomize entirely the true meaning of project success. This project was completed at 1,300 percent above the original budget and took 10 years longer than planned to construct! However, it is considered one of the most popular tourist attractions in the world, attracting more than 10.9 million people a year (it has been added to UNESCO's world heritage list). It has continued to generate huge revenue for its investors with the landmark becoming not just an asset of huge economic value but of culturally priceless significance for the people of Australia. Therefore, despite failing at a project level, the Sydney Opera House project has been a marvelous success at an operational, business, and strategic level in the long run.

Additionally, the use of a multidimensional approach for assessing project success at different points in time is considered a useful approach to assess the success of projects at the project management level as well as at the success of the project to the organization strategically. A multidimensional evaluation of project success, according to Zwikael and Meridith (2021), will enhance performance evaluation of projects by distinguishing between

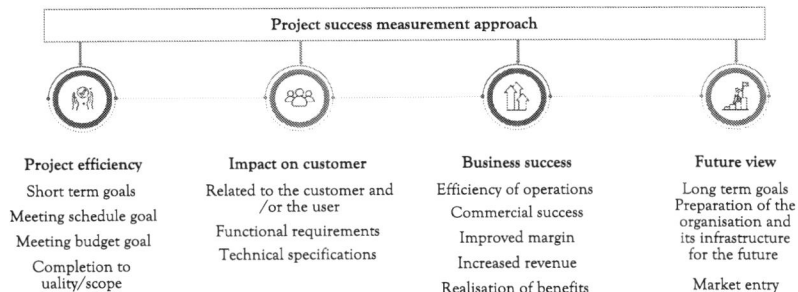

Project success measurement approach			
Project efficiency	**Impact on customer**	**Business success**	**Future view**
Short term goals	Related to the customer and /or the user	Efficiency of operations	Long term goals
Meeting schedule goal		Commercial success	Preparation of the organisation and its infrastructure for the future
Meeting budget goal	Functional requirements	Improved margin	
Completion to uality/scope	Technical specifications	Increased revenue	
		Realisation of benefits	Market entry

Figure 1.3 Example of a dimensional approach to project success measurement

Source: Shenhar, Dvir, Lever, and Maltz 2001

the short- and long-term results. Figure 1.3 shows a classical example of the multidimensional approach to project success measurement.

Figure 1.3 shows that time-dependent project success is divided into four dimensions. The first dimensions measure the efficiency of the project during execution and after completion of a project. The second dimension measures the performance level after the project has been delivered to the client. The third dimension is focused on the contribution of the project to the business and achievement of the benefits the project was set out to achieve such as efficiency gains, revenue generation, improvement in margin, and so on. The fourth dimension is used to measure the success of the project after a period of time (e.g., two or three years) after completion of the project.

Therefore, a multidimensional approach to project success measurement in addition to a multistakeholder view of project success is recommended. This will enable measurement of success of the project at the right level of analysis, from the right perspective using the relevant success metric and at the right time horizon/stage of the overall project life cycle.

Need for This Book

This book was written following the author's experience for more than 20 years in the field of project control, project management, commercial management, academia, and major projects advisory and consultancy across many industries as well as carrying out a PhD (Doctor of Philosophy) research into project control practice in the UK (see the section titled "Overview of the Research Underpinning the project control inhibitors management (PCIM) Methodology and Applicability of This Book" later in this chapter for an overview of the research). The reason for the research and then this book is that most research in relation to project delivery success have focused generally on the causes of cost and time overrun and project success factors. These usually only provide a view of the superficial aspect of factors that can enable project success without focusing on inhibitors and factors that need to be controlled. Consequently, much of the guidance available to project control practitioners have focused mainly on general project management practice with project control usually getting a passing mention. The implication of this is that there is a general lack of guidance on issues surrounding the execution of project controls in practice and how practitioners can deal with the factors that may inhibit effective project control in practice.

Additionally, project control is also discussed generally in pockets of either techniques such as critical path method (CPM), earned value management (EVM), performance evaluation and review technique (PERT), cost-value reconciliation, and so on (see Chapters 7 and 8 for more on these techniques) or software packages such as Microsoft Project, Asta Powerproject, Primavera P6, and so on. Project control is rarely discussed as a whole practice, but these techniques and software packages in isolation do not form the project control system or practice. There are other issues that combine with these techniques and software tools to constitute the project control practice of a project or an organization. Some of these issues include how the techniques and software packages are deployed, the organizational environment where project control is implemented, the planning and estimating process, and the factors that hinder or support project controls. The author's view is that there is a lack of a comprehensive project control framework that considers the whole project control system with recommended good practices for all aspects of the project control process.

Furthermore, most books related to project control have been devoted to explaining project control concepts, tools, and techniques but not the factors that make it difficult to use these tools and techniques in practice. This book focuses on addressing these shortcomings by presenting a project control framework that looks at project control as a system affected by factors and develops mitigation for these identified project control inhibitors. The book also concentrates on guiding practitioners on how to implement project control successfully by providing good practices for various aspects of the project control process. Additionally, one of the most important advantages of using this book is that it not only focuses on cost, time, and scope control, concepts, and application in practice, but it also goes into a great detail on the enabling environment in practice to achieve effective project control. This book is filled with practical best practices that can be used during the project control process.

Introduction to the PCIM Methodology for Effective Project Control

To enable the implementation of a comprehensive project control practice, it is important to consider the project, the project control process/cycle, project control techniques, and software tools as well as the environment where project control is taking place. The PCIM methodology has been developed to achieve a comprehensive and integrated view of project control practice. The PCIM project control approach is described in detail in Chapters 4 to 6 with reference made to it all through this book; however, it is introduced in this section to provide readers with an overview.

The underlying hypothesis of the PCIM project control methodology is that the project control process is not a closed system and is affected by factors in the environment where the project is taking place and the controls environment of the organization. Furthermore, the PCIM asserts that even with the most sophisticated project control techniques and tools, there will be inhibitors to the project control effort. This is because projects do not take place in isolation and are affected by the wider environment. Therefore, the PCIM project control methodology hypothesis is that to control a project successfully, it is important to recognize the need to identify and manage the factors that inhibit project practitioners from effective project control. The PCIM methodology framework is depicted by Figure 1.4. The PCIM project control methodology is focused on the following aspects:

- The project phases, which are the primary phases through which a project proceeds (planning, execution, and completion) and are depicted by the top section in the PCIM framework;
- The primary project control steps (monitor, report, analyze, feedback, action, and revise plan), depicted as the middle section of the PCIM framework;
- The factors that inhibit effective project control (in essence, the environment under which project control is implemented and reflect the fact that project control is not a closed system and is often inhibited by some factors), depicted as the bottom section of the PCIM framework.

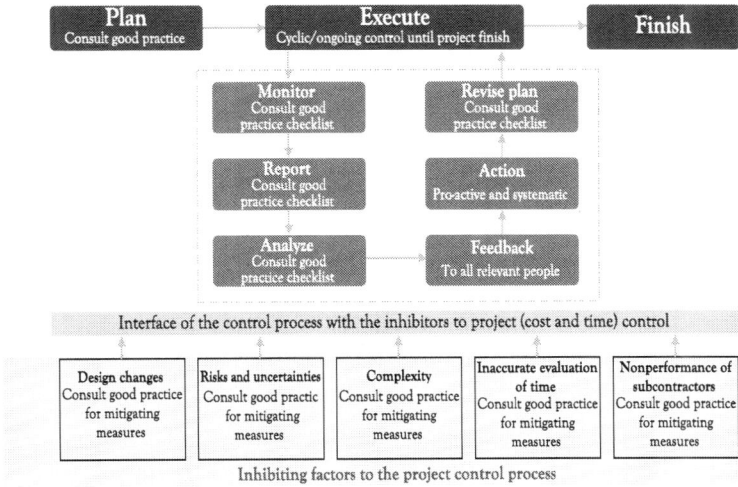

Plan
Consult good practice

Execute
Cyclic/ongoing control until project finish

Finish

Monitor
Consult good
practice checklist

Revise plan
Consult good
practice checklist

Report
Consult good
practice checklist

Action
Pro-active and systematic

Analyze
Consult good
practice checklist

Feedback
To all relevant people

Interface of the control process with the inhibitors to project (cost and time) control

| Design changes Consult good practice for mitigating measures | Risks and uncertainties Consult good practic for mitigating measures | Complexity Consult good practice for mitigating measures | Inaccurate evaluation of time Consult good practice for mitigating measures | Nonperformance of subcontractors Consult good practice for mitigating measures |

Inhibiting factors to the project control process

Figure 1.4 PCIM methodology framework

It is important to note that the PCIM project control methodology is not just superficial, but it includes several good practices that can be used to manage and mitigate each of these project control inhibitors (see Chapter 5) as well as good practices to support practitioners through the major steps of the cyclical project control process (planning, monitoring, reporting, and analyzing) (see Chapter 6). Finally, the PCIM project control methodology is not rigid, it is flexible and scalable as the methodology underpinning it can be used as a blueprint and adapted for projects in various industries or countries.

Overview of the Research Underpinning the PCIM Methodology and Applicability of This Book

As stated previously, the PCIM project control methodology emanated from a PhD research on project control practice that was carried out over a five-year time frame in the UK. The doctoral research followed a rigorous three-stage process (as shown in the Figure 1.5) that utilized a combination of quantitative and qualitative methodology, and a range of research methods.

Literature analysis
Identify factors that can potentially inhibit effective project cost and time

Stage One

Quantitative study
Questionnaire survey and analysis
Determine top inhibitor of project control practice

Qualitative study
Interviews and literature review
Capture knowledge, reflection and experience of project control practitioners and evaluate recommendations on project planning and control

Stage Two

Analysis and synthesis
Analyse and synthesise transcripts and literature

Develop project control framework
Develop a framework that can be used for the cost and time control process

Develop a checklist of good practice
Develop and Categories a list of mitigating measure

Stage Three

Evaluate and improve framework/checklist using delphi process
Analyse and synthesise transcripts and literature

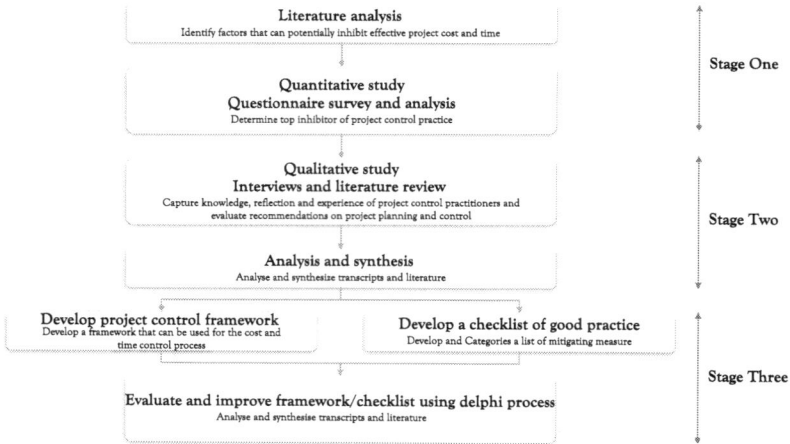

Figure 1.5 The PCIM project control methodology research process

First Stage: Literature Analysis and Quantitative Study

The first stage of the research was used to establish the top inhibitors of project cost and time control practice. By initially using a literature analysis of hundreds of empirical research studies, many factors that can potentially inhibit effective cost and time control were identified. After which a questionnaire survey was used to establish the leading factors that hamper practitioners from controlling effectively the cost and time objectives of their project in practice and to obtain information on project cost and time control practice in the UK construction project industry. The questionnaires were administered to 250 construction project organizations in the UK by company turnover/company fee earnings and completed by highly experienced construction project practitioners within these organizations. The analysis of the returned questionnaires showed that 64 percent of the responding practitioners were construction project contractors who had more than 25 years of experience and 69 percent of responding practitioners were construction project consultancies that had more than 25 years of experience.

Second Stage: Qualitative Study (Interviews) and Synthesis

The second stage of the PCIM research process utilized semistructured interviews to explore the topical issues revealed by the questionnaire survey and unveiled further, the experiences of practitioners in relation to project control in depth. The same sample of companies used for the survey stage of the research was used. A total of 15 companies offered relevant project practitioners for interviews, ranging from construction directors, project directors, commercial directors, to senior project managers. Most of the interviewees were experienced employees of their companies (construction project contractors and construction project consultancies). The total professional experience of the 15 interviewees was 402 years (an average experience of nearly 27 years).

Third Stage: PCIM Project Control Methodology Development, Evaluation, and Refinement

The PCIM framework and methodology development process commenced at this stage by first modeling the results of the analysis carried out during the first two stages of the research to produce an initial preliminary framework for project cost and time control. The preliminary framework was refined iteratively based on synthesis of the findings and analysis of the questionnaire survey, interviews, the author's experience, and further literature analysis. Several good practices were also developed to support the various aspects of the PCIM framework (to form the PCIM project control methodology). The PCIM project control methodology was then presented to construction project practitioners for evaluation and validation using the Delphi technique, a systematic technique that enables experts to reach a consensus on various opinions (see Chapter 6 for more on the Delphi process). The Delphi process helped generate more input to further improve the PCIM methodology, validate the model and develop a good practice checklist, and to reach a consensus on the significance of each of the practices.

Applicability of This Book to Different Industries

Finally, although the research underpinning the PCIM project control methodology was conducted in the UK construction and infrastructure project industry, the author has endeavored to make this book useful to readers from other industries. Many of the chapters of this book cover general project control topics that are applicable to many industries.

Additionally, the author has many years of experience of working and consulting on projects in many industrial sectors (such as financial services, IT, facilities management, pharmaceutical, academia, construction, government, energy, telecom, consultancy, and so on). Therefore, the author has used his diverse experiences across these sectors to influence the content of this book.

Organization and Overview of This Book

This book is a two-part applied book organized into 12 chapters. The first part of the book (Chapters 2 to 6) is focused on how to achieve effective controls using the PCIM project control methodology and accompanying good practices. The second part of the book (Chapters 7 to 12) is on the classical and general techniques used during project control followed by the concluding chapter. The content of each of the chapters is described below.

Part One: Achieving Effective Project Controls Using the PCIM Project Control Methodology

Chapter 1: Introduction

This chapter provides a background to the book by first introducing the concept of project control and its importance during projects. The reasons for utilizing project control are followed by an explanation of what is meant by project success and the approaches that can be used to view project success. The chapter then goes on to explain the rationale for the book. This is followed by an introduction to the PCIM project control methodology followed by an overview of the research that informed its development.

Chapter 2: Fundamental Concepts of Project Control

The theory and key concepts that underpin project control are presented and discussed. The chapter starts by explaining the relationship between project control and project management, followed by an explanation of the types of project control and articulation of the classical factors controlled in a project. The chapter concludes with a detailed discussion of the project control cycle including its constituent steps.

Chapter 3: Project Control in Practice and Prevention of Challenges to Effective Project Control

This chapter provides an overview of project control in practice including the prevailing time and cost control practices, including their shortcomings. The chapter also accentuates one of the hypotheses of the PCIM project control methodology by asserting that project control does not operate in a vacuum and demonstrates this by providing insights into the day-to-day barriers that make effective project cost and time control challenging from a practitioner's perspective. Several good practices that can be used by practitioners to deal with these challenges are also recommended.

Chapter 4: Using the Project Control Inhibitors Management (PCIM) Methodology to Improve Project Control in Practice

This chapter emphasizes the fact that project control is not just about utilization of a technique, but that it is a complex process that requires human interventions, decisions, and practices, and the process is usually inhibited by many factors. The project control inhibitors management (PCIM) framework is presented and discussed as an approach that can be used to manage projects more effectively. The process and thinking used in the development of the PCIM project control approach is also discussed.

Chapter 5: Good Practices to Mitigate the Foremost Project Cost and Time Control Inhibitors

This chapter starts by reinforcing one of the hypotheses of the PCIM project control methodology: project cost and time control will be more effective if project control processes in organizations are accompanied by practices to enable success. To this effect, the foremost project cost and time control inhibitors are discussed and classified as well as an overview of the research that identified them. Furthermore, 100 good practices that can be deployed during project control to mitigate the foremost cost and time control inhibitors are presented and discussed.

Chapter 6: Good Practices for the Cyclic Project Control Steps; Planning, Monitoring, Reporting, and Analyzing

The chapter presents a set of 65 good practices for the major steps of the project control cycle (planning, monitoring, reporting, and analyzing). This chapter also reports on the Delphi process that was conducted to evaluate, validate, and obtain consensus on the significance of each of the developed good practices for the key steps of the project control cycle.

Part Two: Classical Techniques Used During Project Control

Chapter 7: Classical Project Time Control Techniques

This chapter presents and describes the various project time control techniques such as Gantt bar chart, line of balance (LOB), CPM, program evaluation, and review technique and others. The chapter also provides an assessment of these techniques to reveal their applicability, advantages, and shortcomings.

Chapter 8: Classical Project Cost Control Techniques

This chapter presents and describes the various project cost control techniques such as unit and standard costing, cost and value reconciliation, EVM, and others. The chapter also provides an assessment of these techniques to reveal their applicability, advantages, and shortcomings.

Chapter 9: Project Scope Management

This chapter presents and describes the scope management process and discusses concepts like scope initiation, scope planning, scope control, and the work breakdown structure (WBS). It concludes by highlighting good practices in relation to scope control on projects.

Chapter 10: Risk Management

This chapter presents a detailed explanation of the risk management process including the subprocesses of risk identification, risk analysis, (including some relevant qualitative and quantitative techniques), and risk response. Concepts such as risk categorisation, risk classification, risk tolerance and risk appetite are also discussed.

Chapter 11: Overview of Supplier Performance Management, Business Case, and Benefit Management Processes

This chapter starts by focusing on some of the key project management processes that are important for and support project control. An overview of supplier performance management, the business case process, and benefits management are provided.

Chapter 12: Ingredients of an Effective Project Control Environment

The book ends by discussing the key ingredients for an effective project control environment and argues that these should be put in place by organizations to give their project control effort the best chance of success.

PART 1

Achieving Effective Project Controls Using the PCIM Project Control Methodology

CHAPTER 2

Fundamental Concepts of Project Control

What Is Project Control?

Projects are usually executed on a budgeted capital and therefore are required to be completed within the available capital. Projects are also typically required for a purpose and therefore need to be completed before a deadline and to an agreed scope so that they can be utilized for the purpose intended. The need to complete a project within a capital budget, to a required scope, and delivery by a specified date point inherently to cost, scope, and time being arguably the most important objectives of most projects. Delivery of projects within a monetary budget, to an agreed scope, and by a specified date then become constraints imposed on projects. The financial constraint demands that the project costs be controlled (cost control) and the delivery by a specified date will require that the time expended on a project be controlled (time control). The successful control of cost and time requires scope control.

Cost control, scope control, and time control are important in projects so that cost overrun, scope creep, and time overrun are prevented. However, delivering projects within their cost estimates and on time has been considered to be challenging. There are many accounts of projects overrunning their cost and time. The seminal Egan (1998) report in the UK sums this up by stating that "projects are widely seen as unpredictable in terms of delivery on time, within budget." The management tool for facilitating the predictability and completion of projects on time and within budget is "control." Generally, controlling is an integral part of management with the function of management usually described as planning, organizing, leading, and controlling. Similarly, in the project context, control is also one of the major tools of project management;

this is apparent from most definitions of project management where control always gets a mention. For example, the APM defined project management classically in its *Body of Knowledge* (BoK), 5th edition, as the process by which projects are defined, planned, monitored, controlled, and delivered such that the agreed benefits are derived. In fact, it can be argued that the role of the project manager during the execution phase mainly revolves around monitoring and controlling the project to enable successful delivery.

The Concept of Project Control

In a bid to discuss the issue of project control, it will be appropriate to start the discussion from the body of knowledge known as project management. Project management arose from the need to manage projects. Project management differs from the normal day-to-day management of businesses and organizations. A project is a unique, transient endeavor undertaken to bring about change and to achieve the planned objectives (APM 2019) with the intention of completing the project within a specified time, cost, and to a required quality standard.

What then is project management? Project management has existed informally for many centuries since the ancient projects we know of, such as the pyramids of Giza, Colosseum, Great Wall of China, would have relied on some of the principles of modern-day project management such as planning, monitoring, control, and so on to complete these projects successfully. However, modern project management is a relatively new field of management that evolved in recent decades in a bid to manage the set objectives of a project and associated activities effectively. Therefore, the Project Management Institute (2021) in the United States has defined project management as the "application of knowledge, skills, tools, and techniques to project activities to meet the project requirements." The APM (2010) in the UK has similarly described project management as the process by which projects are defined, planned, monitored, controlled, and delivered such that the agreed benefits are realized. Effective project management requires planning, measuring, evaluating, forecasting, and controlling all aspects of a project including quality and quantity of work, costs, and time. It is evident that controlling is a major part of project management. The aim of controlling is to ensure that the future that is desired from a plan comes to fruition. Therefore, since projects are manifestations of the future of a past plan, the need for control in achieving that plan is crucial. The reality is that the objectives of a project would rarely be met on time and within budget unless the project is controlled in such a way that the deviations from plans are detected and corrected in a timely manner.

Factors That Are Controlled in a Project

Traditionally, the most important control areas in a project include the following:

- Control of time;
- Control of cost;
- Control of scope and quality (scope in this book will be taken as including quality because the scope of a project includes the specification of quality required);
- Control of procurement and supply;
- Control of logistics; and
- Control of resources.;

However, from the above, three factors, namely, time, cost, and scope, are regarded as the fundamental areas requiring control in a project. So important are these that classical project management literature has referred to cost, time, and quality as the "iron triangle," first proposed by Dr. Martin Barnes in 1969 (Zwikael and Meridith 2021) or the triple constraints of projects as discussed in the next section.

The Triple Constraints

As mentioned previously, the most common areas needing control are cost, time, and quality/scope (the triple constraints). From the onset of project management, successful project execution and the ultimate objective in project management has been about achieving the performance

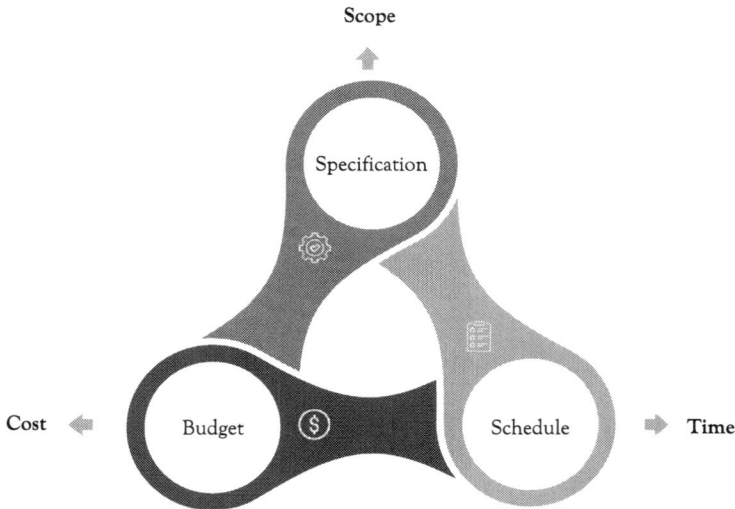

Figure 2.1 The triple constraints of project management

specifications (scope and quality) on or before the time schedule and within the budgeted cost. This constitutes the triple constraints (Figure 2.1).

For the project to be successful, the three constraints would have to be controlled effectively. Therefore, the emphasis of project control is usually on the following:

- *Time* (progress): The aim of time control is to keep the progress of the project on schedule and minimize time overruns.
- *Cost*: Cost control monitors how much is spent on the project against budgets to highlight and explain variances, control cost increase, prevent unauthorized expenditures, and update the cost baselines with the forecast cost to completion.
- *Scope*: The aim of scope and change control is to facilitate the governance of change to the scope of the project including allowing only the necessary changes and approval. Scope control also includes quality control, which covers the management of the work contained in the scope to achieve the desired requirements and specifications avoiding/minimizing errors and mistakes.

Type of Project Controls

There are three basic types of controls as described below:

- *Cybernetic control,* which is self-regulatory automatic control that operates in a closed system that uses a self-correcting feedback loop for the control. By this, we mean measurements are taken by the system and sent automatically for comparison against some predetermined performance requirements. If deviations from the performance requirements are found, the system then acts automatically to correct the deviation. The common thermostat is a good example of this.
- *Go/no-go controls* are not automatic. However, like the cybernetic control, they also involve the use of predetermined performance standards where another entity that is inside or outside the system tests the current performance of the system against some predetermined performance standards usually at regular, periodic intervals. Most of the controls in project management fall into this category. However, because the check is not automatic and happens periodically, it also allows errors to build up before they are identified at the next check.
- *Postcontrol* is also known as postperformance controls, reviews, or postproject controls or reviews. It is applied after the project, but it is not a vain attempt to alter what has already occurred. It is directed at improving the chances for future projects to meet their goals.

In a project-specific environment when the activities of a project are not progressing as planned, then action is taken normally. The actions are focused on a single exclusive objective of bringing the project back in line with its schedule or cost budget. There are two ways of implementing the control needed. These are as follows:

- *Feedback control:* This type of control monitors the output from the activities of a project and then adjusts the input to the activities as necessary to achieve a desired performance output (see Figure 2.2). The risk of this approach is that

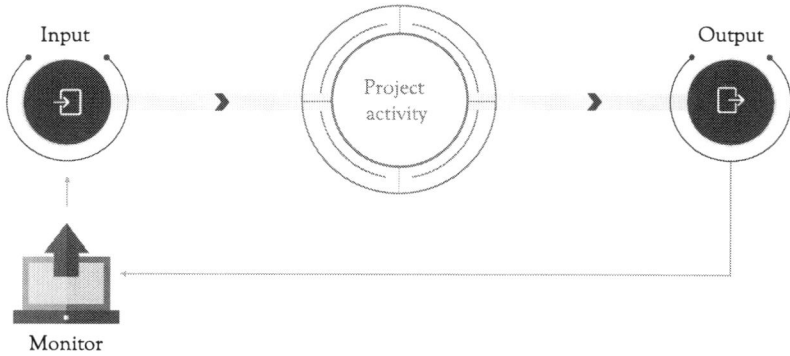

Figure 2.2 Feedback control system

unless instantaneous feedback is obtained, the system may not produce information quickly enough to allow action. In order words, it is a reactive control. Ironically, feedback control is the most common form of control utilized for projects. That is, where project reports of all areas of the project are produced or obtained, performance is then analyzed against the set standard and then corrective actions are taken as appropriate.

• *Feed-forward control*: This is applicable for activities and project operations where what is happening is well understood. Feed-forward control involves the monitoring of the input to an activity before it starts or as the activity is ongoing and compared not with the output of that activity, but with the input required to achieve a desired output. The input is then adjusted accordingly impacting the desired output of the activity in question (see Figure 2.3). The feed-forward control is a proactive and active control process. That is, on projects, the feed-forward control consists of checking proactively the plan for an activity against the plan that will achieve the desired output. Where inadequacies are found, control actions are then taken by adjusting the planned input, for example, increasing the level of resources required for that activity. In essence, this control is performed on an activity before that activity is carried out or as it is progressing.

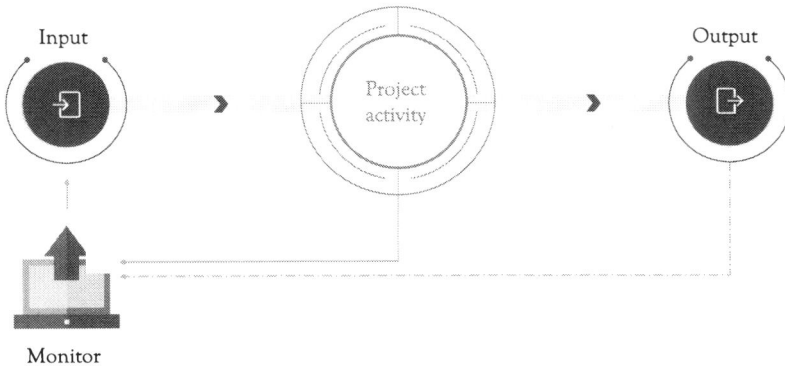

Figure 2.3 Feed-forward control system

Project Control Cycle and Steps

The project control cycle involves planning, implementing the plan, monitoring actual output, and recording it, reporting actual as well as planned parameters and their variations, and finally taking corrective action.

It is important to note that project control is not a one-time event; it is like driving a car to a planned destination. However, to reach the destination successfully, the driver needs to be in control all through the journey, following the key steps of driving a car and the rules of the road. On a project, the process of project control is a continuous feedback loop right from the conception of the project through to completion. However, this continuous feedback process is usually achieved in four phases: (1) setting planned performance standards, (2) comparing these planned standards with actual performance and forecast future results, (3) reporting the results as appropriate, and then (4) taking required corrective action as appropriate to recover or minimize the deviation from planned performance to return the project to the desired position or as close to it as possible. A typical project control cycle is shown in Figure 2.4.

In practice, the project control steps will usually involve the following:

1. The definition of the performance standards planned for a project traditionally will be the "iron triangle" explained earlier (budgeted cost, time, and scope/quality specifications), but more recently other

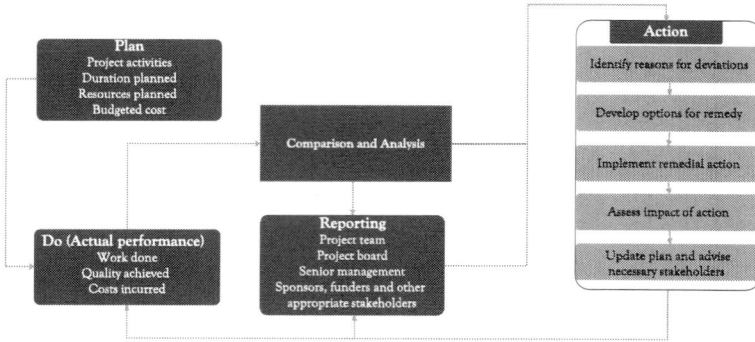

Figure 2.4 Typical project control cycle

performance standards are considered such as stakeholder satisfaction, resource requirements, sustainability, usability, and so on as explained in the section titled "When has a Project Performed Successfully?" in chapter one.

2. Then, these performance standards are compared with the actual project performance to date. Schedule, cost budgets, and scope are compared to the progress of work, associated cost, and achieved scope. The remaining time to deliver the work and necessary cost of work remaining are then established and used to forecast the completion date of the project and outturn cost.

3. Reports are produced to present the outcome of this comparison, which are then shared with the appropriate internal and external project stakeholders.

4. Finally, whenever actual performance deviates significantly from the planned performance standards, corrective actions are taken as appropriate to bring the project back on track if possible or minimize the impact.

The main steps to the project control process as outlined above are discussed in more detail in the following sections.

Planning

Planning and controlling are like "twins" in the project implementation process. This is because planning cannot achieve success without control while control itself could not be done without plans. Although planning and control are usually used together as a project management tool, they are quite distinct, with planning being a step within the project control process. Broadly, planning refers to the establishment of the goals and objectives of a future task or ongoing task (in the case of replanning), the setting out of the associated activities making up the task, the procedures, and the resources required to carry out these activities. Principally, planning is the setting out of what must be done and how to meet one or more objectives before proceeding to act in accordance with what has been set out. The plan captures in one concise document what needs to be done and the delivery approach. The plan documents all the material aspects relating to the delivery of a project including objectives, strategic approach, resources, cost, timeline, key milestones, and so on. Project planning is the modeling of a project, comprising the documentation of how the triple constraints (as discussed in the section titled "*The Triple Constraints*" *earlier* and shown in Figure 2.1) will be satisfied.

More specifically, project planning is basically planning in a project environment, with the APM (2015) describing project planning as the process of identifying the methods, resources, and activities necessary to accomplish the project objectives. Therefore, project planning involves the development of multiple plans: for the scope and performance dimension (the WBS), schedule dimension (preferably a network diagram), cost dimension (a financial estimate), and so on. The section below provides an overview of the project plan and its content.

Project Plan and Its Content

A project plan has often been confused with a project schedule, but it is worthwhile to note that while a project schedule and program are often called project plans by some practitioners, a project plan is not a project schedule. This is because a project schedule usually lays out project tasks and timings and enables the monitoring and controlling of progress as work proceeds, but the project plan contains the project schedule, and a lot more besides such as implementation strategy, configuration management, organization roles and responsibilities, and so on, as shown in Table 2.1. Project plans aid coordination and communication and help avoid problems during the execution of projects.

Table 2.1 Typical content of a project plan

Section	Typical contents
Project summary	An overview of the project including background information on the project and the key particulars and information about the project.
Project objectives and requirements	Describe what the project sets out to achieve as contained in the business case and the key specifications, features, **and** performance standards of the project that need to be met.
Approach	A detailed explanation of how the project will be implemented including any methodology and procedures that will be followed.
Timeline and milestones	An outline of the overall timescale for delivering the project with important milestones clearly stated.
Scope	Information on the boundary of what the project is delivering including setting out of scope area for the project, especially those that stakeholders might logically consider part of the project but are not within scope of the project (for example, work being delivered by another project or which will be delivered as part of a future phase).
Configuration management	The approach that will be used to manage the creation and control of the various aspects of the tasks, outputs, and scope of work required to deliver the project.
Dependencies	Documentation of things, decisions, other projects, and others that the project relies on to start, progress, or complete. This will include internal and external dependencies.
Resource needs	A summary of all the resources that are required to complete the project.
Roles and responsibilities	An outline of the project roles and responsibilities, which could also include a RACI matrix.
Assumptions and constraints	A list of the assumptions that have been used in planning the project as well as any limitations that the project needs to work within.
Schedule	A diagrammatic depiction of the activities and tasks that will be delivered to achieve the project including their timing, sequencing, and interdependency relationships.
Cost	A document of the cost estimate for executing the project, overall budget, and how cost will be managed during the project.
Risk and issue management	Documentation of the key risks of the project, their analysis, and mitigation/management approach and a log of the current issues and how they will be managed.
Quality management	A description of processes that will be used to monitor and control the outputs and works to deliver the project so that they meet the performance and quality specifications agreed for the outputs, works, and overall project.
Deployment and implementation approach	Explanation of the entry into service strategy for the completed project including how the completed project will be implemented such as timeline and phasing if applicable.

Project Execution Plan

The project execution plan (PEP) is a document that establishes how the execution of a project will be managed to completion. The PEP describes how the overall execution phase of a project will be managed to meet the requirements of the project. In documenting how the various aspects of a project's execution phase will be managed, the PEP usually incorporates the roles and responsibilities of the project's parties in relation to the project as well as their relationships with each other.

The PEP usually starts by providing the project background and the project objectives. The resource levels required to execute the project as well as the delivery timeline are also contained in the PEP. The PEP also presents the communication and consultation procedure required for the project as well as the stakeholder management plan. The PEP also describes the governance arrangement for the project during the execution stage including the policies and procedures that will be adopted. For example, the PEP will usually have a risk section that explains the agreed approach for risk management including details of the risk governance and reporting structure within the project. Table 2.2 provides an example of the content of the PEP.

Table 2.2 Contents of a PEP

- Project definition and a summary of the strategic brief or later the project brief
- Roles, responsibilities, and relationships
- Design drawings
- Government authority approvals, permissions, and consents approach
- Project schedule
- Cost plan, cost management procedures
- Risk management strategy
- Issue management plan
- Contracting and procurement strategy
- Monitoring and reporting strategy
- Stakeholder management plan
- Gateway review process: internal and external/funders (if appropriate)
- Communication plan
- Technology strategy
- Change management approach
- Health and safety strategy
- Sustainability strategy
- Quality assurance strategy
- Handover and project acceptance approach

Monitoring and Reporting

When performance standards have been set through planning, the next step in the project control process is usually to monitor and report on actual performance. Monitoring is the process that provides information on all aspects of a project so that management can use the information to understand the status of the project based on deliberate actions as well as unplanned or unforeseen events on the project. Monitoring aims to determine whether the intended objectives have been met. In a project environment, monitoring involves the process that facilitates the checking and validation of a project's performance metrics and comparison with the planned and predicted project's metrics. The aim of project monitoring is to ascertain whether the project is progressing in accordance with the project's plan while providing information that can then be used to forecast the possible status of the project in the future.

Reporting is closely intertwined with monitoring, but reporting is the communication aspect of monitoring. Reporting provides an account of the work accomplished at a stated date (usually the reporting period end date) and information on the predicted project's key performance including cost and schedule. Reporting also highlights current and potential problems identified during monitoring and presents the management action underway to overcome the effects of the problems. The importance of effective and accurate reporting in the project control process cannot be overemphasized because the report is where the information collected during monitoring is contained and it is an analysis of the information that shows the status of the project.

The PCIM project control methodology research that informed this book has developed best practices for the monitoring and reporting steps of the project control process. These are presented in Chapter 6.

Analysis (Comparison and Evaluation)

After monitoring and reporting, the next step in project cost and time control is the analysis of the cost and time information contained in the submitted report. Having gathered the data, the team must determine whether the project is behaving as predicted, and if not, calculate the size and impact of the variances. The quantitative measures of progress are time, scope, and cost and so they receive significant attention during the project control process. The project control team will utilize the reports to forecast time and cost at completion and compute any difference (variance) between these figures and the baseline. The data and information from the monitoring process are then evaluated for any trends that may impact the performance of the project. Following this, analysis of the project's progress is done to determine the effect of the latest reported and evaluated information on the project's planned performance objectives. There are many techniques that can be used for the analysis steps of the project control process (details of the available project control techniques are presented in Chapters 7 and 8). However, it is important to point out that the main objective of analysis in project control is to identify proactively, potential negative trends that might hamper the achievement of the project objectives to prevent this negative event from coming to fruition.

The PCIM project control methodology research has also developed best practices for the analysis step of the project control process. These are presented in Chapter 6.

Action

To close the control loop, the team must take effective action to overcome any identified variance and deviation from the set project performance plan. The action step of the project control process is concerned with identifying and evaluating alternative courses of action for resolving a perceived problem situation. The objective of action is the development of a timely plan to mitigate problems affecting the project's performance. To elaborate, the objectives of the action step in project control include the production of a recommended course of action, together with a statement of the implications of the action for the future of the project so that the project team and management will understand the consequential impact of the action should they decide to go for it. In practice, this action step may well involve an element of replanning, for example, carrying out a "what if" analysis that can then be used to evaluate implications for the future of the project.

Action closes the project control loop and if action is not taken when required the whole project control process is in vain. That is, just monitoring a project, knowing the performance, and reporting it to the relevant project stakeholders should not be mistaken with control. The control loop is only closed when appropriate action is taken and then continuing the control cycle by monitoring the impact of the action on the project. Actions need to be cost-effective and proportionate in relation to the issue they have been instigated to solve. Additionally, actions need to be timely so that they achieve their purpose but carried out in a controlled manner so that they do not create additional problems through careless implementation.

CHAPTER 3

Project Control in Practice and Prevention of Challenges to Effective Project Control

Overview of Project Control Process in Practice

The preceding chapter discussed the theoretical concept of project control. Sometimes, theoretical concepts do not align with reality. This chapter explains how project control is implemented in practice and some of the challenges it is exposed to, as well as how to surmount these challenges.

In practice, project control is often a multifaceted task undertaken by managers and practitioners working on projects. As discussed in the previous chapter, project control is a complex and iterative process. It is about the final step in management and during the control stage—the level of performance is compared with the planned objectives to find any deviation and corrective action taken as appropriate.

Research underpinning the project control inhibitors management (PCIM) methodology has identified several challenges and shortcomings of the project cost and time control processes in practice. These are discussed in the remaining sections of this chapter.

Prevalent Project Time Control
in Practice and Shortcomings

Although the research that informed the PCIM methodology was focused on the control of construction and infrastructure projects, the author has supplemented this chapter with his experience of working on other types of projects such as IT projects, research and development projects, transformation projects, consultancy projects, implementation of new financial services policy projects, and so on. The time objectives of projects are controlled by practitioners broadly following a common process. The prevalent time control practice as revealed by the PCIM project control methodology research is depicted in Figure 3.1 and described as follows.

Assessment of Duration of Tasks and Activities

The first step in the project time control process in practice normally involves an assessment of the resources available in the company to establish that there are adequate levels of personnel required to deliver the project. The duration of the project is decided at this stage. The methods for determining the duration of the project revolve around "assessment from experience" and "the use of calculations." One problem with determining the duration of projects at this stage lies in the lack of involvement

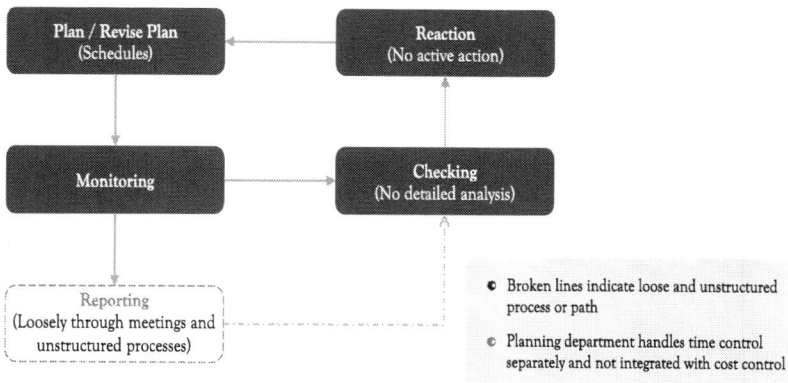

Figure 3.1 Descriptive model of the prevailing time control process in practice

of supply chain partners. Therefore, durations of partners' tasks are based on assumptions, which can sometimes be inaccurate.

Visual Representation of Project Duration

The second step usually involves the development of a visual representation of the project duration, most often using scheduling software packages to produce a graphical output (Gantt or bar charts). Different forms of schedules are developed for different purposes. The different forms of schedules utilized in practice include:

- Tender schedule – which is the proposed schedule for delivering the project when it was tendered;
- Contract schedule – which is the schedule that is part of the signed contract documents and the one the project contractor must deliver to;
- Target schedule – which is a replanned schedule used by management to drive work during project delivery aimed at delivering the project quicker than the current master schedule. Therefore, the contract schedule is not always handed to the construction site team, instead the more ambitious target schedule is utilized;
- Stage schedule – which is a schedule developed for the different stages of the project; and
- Project master schedule – This is the current approved overarching schedule for the project, which has taken account of current change requests and incorporates all the work packages, and has therefore become the latest contract schedule. Schedules can also be referred to by "levels" as below:
- Level 1 schedule is the project's master schedule which presents the key milestones and major activities of the project usually on one page;
- Level 2 schedule is the project management summary schedule which shows the project broken down into its major component including interfaces and used to show the integration of the work required to deliver the project;

- level 3 schedule is the control level schedule which is an integrated schedule of the project and contains all major milestones, procurement, design, execution/delivery, testing etc.;
- Level 4 schedule is the detailed network schedule and the schedule used for the execution of the project;
- Level 5 schedule is a more detailed breakdown of the level 4 schedule and used as a very tactical schedule to manage day-to-day activities of the project usually by supervisors on a short-term basis.

The assessment of duration and visual representation of the preceding project duration steps can be categorized as the planning phase of the project control cycle, the first step of the theoretical project control process.

Monitoring and Reporting of Progress

The third step of project time control in practice is normally monitoring and reporting. However, the PCIM research found that there is usually no dedicated monitoring process in place. Therefore, monitoring is usually ad hoc at best. Consequently, in practice, there is usually no due diligence on monitoring to ensure objectivity, leading to risk of nonfactual information being reported by project-level staff. Furthermore, the research shows that there is no real mechanism in place for reporting progress from the project site to the project/head office. At best, any reporting mechanism in place is often loose and unstructured.

This step of the project time control appears to move straight from monitoring to the analyzing stage bypassing the reporting process. It was found that in practice the reporting phase of project time control is only loosely incorporated into the overall project time control process. Most of the time, it was unclear if time is monitored directly by the project office or progress is reported to the project office by the project-level team. The most common time reporting structure in practice during construction projects is through progress meetings, which usually take place on a weekly basis. In the author's experience (having delivered many projects as well as carried out consultancy performance reviews on dozens of projects), this informal reporting process, such as meetings between the client and the contractor and meetings between the contractor and subcontractors, is practised in most projects. This form of reporting structure is obviously not the most effective because necessary control action may be delayed between the interval of meetings. Meetings should not be discounted as they are a valuable method of discussing issues relating to the project and are often wider than project time control, but they should not be the main time control reporting avenue. Instead, meetings should just serve as a supplementary reporting structure or a high-level reporting forum.

Analysis

The fourth step in the prevailing project time control process in practice is the analysis of the information acquired through monitoring and reporting (albeit loose and unstructured). In practice, the use of robust project control analysis techniques like earned value analysis is not widespread, the prevailing practice when analyzing during time control is a qualitative evaluation of the current progress against the planned progress by marking progress on the project schedules (usually Gantt chart) to check if the project is ahead or behind schedule. This indicated that the Gantt chart doubled up as the time control tool in addition to being used as a scheduling tool. Hence what happens during the "analysis step" of the prevailing project time control process in practice is hardly analysis but interpretation. Interpretation is a very simplistic way of analysis during time control because this technique will hardly reveal the underlying reason for lack of progress or any problem lurking in the project that the project team should be wary of.

Action

The fifth and final step of the project time control process in practice, as customary with most control processes, is "action." It was found that in practice, this appears to be another underutilized aspect of the project time control process. This is because the information generated from the previous step (analysis) is only interpretation and quantitative analytical tools are rarely utilized to reveal future trends. Hence, in practice, corrective actions to bring a project that is behind schedule back on track are quite often only reactive and usually end up not being effective.

Prevalent Project Cost Control in Practice and Shortcomings

The cost control processes for construction projects utilized by practitioners who were involved in the research underpinning the PCIM project control methodology were also found to be common and similar to the author's experience of working on other types of projects such as IT projects, research and development projects, transformation projects, consultancy projects, implementation of new financial services policy projects, and so on. The prevailing cost control process is shown in Figure 3.2 and discussed in the following section.

Cost Estimation

When there is a requirement for a new construction project, the first step is the estimating department is asked to price the job and prepare the estimate. However, quite often, no quantitative estimating method is used. The total project cost estimate is usually developed by obtaining quotations from subcontractors and suppliers for the various work

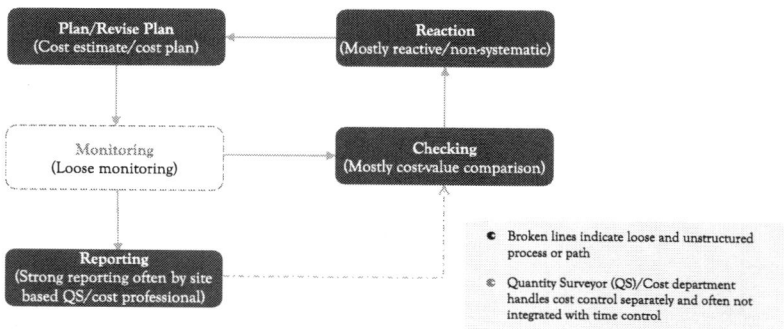

Figure 3.2 Descriptive model of the prevailing cost control process in practice

packages of the project. After the tenders have been priced, a common practice is to ensure that every item, service, or package in the tender has a cost allocated to it in the hope that this will help control the cost of the package during implementation. For projects other than those of construction, for example IT projects, the cost estimating process is similar if the project is to be outsourced. However, for projects that are delivered internally by the company, the cost estimation for the projects takes into account the time to be expended by the various professionals (IT architects, business analysts, solution designers, project managers, and others involved in the project) who will be working on the project and the cost equivalent of these staff or how much will be paid to them if they are brought in as contractors into the business is calculated.

Monitoring of Cost

During project cost control, the second step involves monitoring and, as was the case during control of time, no clear distinction between monitoring and reporting appears to exist in the prevalent project cost control process in practice, although the reversal was noticed (reporting was more structured but monitoring was slack, which was the opposite for time control). During cost control, the monitoring regime in place is not usually robust enough because quite often, monitoring does not follow a periodic regime or utilize a dedicated structure such as computer tools or templates. For other projects such as internal IT projects, the monitoring of cost is even looser and reactive with the cost expended on projects usually extracted from the payment systems by the finance department and may sometimes not be able to be disaggregated easily from the many projects taking place within an organization. For consultancy projects, monitoring of cost is stronger since the services of people are what is usually being sold, time expended on projects is usually recorded on a system with the time expended for each resource, and the associated rate usually used to obtain the current project cost. The cost is usually compared against the agreed fee for the project if it is a fixed-fee consultancy project. If it is a time-based fee, the client is usually advised of the current project cost on a periodic basis such as weekly for comparison against the budget fee.

Reporting of Cost

From the loose monitoring of project cost, the next step revealed involves reporting. As previously mentioned, the reporting mechanism during cost control in practice seems more robust than the monitoring regime. Research informing the PCIM project control methodology found that quite often the monitoring step is bypassed, moving straight from planning (determination of the project cost estimate) to cost reporting. This is because many practitioners alluded to the fact that they have site-based/project-level quantity surveyors (construction project cost professionals) tasked mainly with reporting cost to the project office. The project team rarely completes cost documents since anything to do with cost is considered strictly a quantity-surveying matter. Cost reporting was found to be more robust than cost monitoring on other types of projects as well; for example, in internal IT projects, the costs of resources expended are obtained from the financial system and reported to management periodically such as monthly. However, the project team on ground rarely has a cost-reporting responsibility. The cost-reporting responsibilities are usually the preserve of more senior project staff such as the project manager, and the project director discusses the cost of the project as compiled by the finance department at senior-level meetings such as program and project board meetings with the functional management of the organization.

Analysis of Cost Performance

The fourth step after reporting is analysis, but, unlike the prevailing time control process where interpretation is the norm rather than analysis, there is a wide usage of quantitative analytical tools and techniques for cost control. Practitioners control cost by considering cost and value, using tools like cost–value comparison and earned value analysis (albeit less frequently) to reveal overspend and its causes. Similarly, for other types of projects, cost is usually analyzed. For example, in internal IT projects, the finance department will usually obtain the cost of the projects from the finance system and analyze the cost of the projects. For process engineering projects, analysis of cost is also carried out in detail; here, cost of projects will typically be obtained from the finance system on a periodic (usually monthly) basis. This cost is then supplemented with cost information supplied by the cost professional responsible for the projects, usually called the cost engineer or cost controller. The costs of the projects are then analyzed by this cost professional utilizing techniques such as S-curves, cost of work done and value of work done analysis, anticipated final cost forecast, earned value analysis such as schedule performance index and cost performance index, and so on (cost analysis techniques are discussed in Chapter 8).

Action

The fifth and final step revealed for project cost control is "action" to control potential cost overrun. Although the analysis step is more detailed than was noticed in time control, there was no systematic way of acting when analysis showed the need for action. The PCIM project control methodology research showed that when analysis shows any cost over-run on an activity or work package in construction projects, the prevalent action involved having a meeting with the relevant subcontractor for the area with cost overrun to discuss the issue and how to mitigate the cost overrun or trying to manage the impact on the overall project by shuffling cost by finding other work package(s) with an underspend and reallocating the overrun cost to them. For other types of projects like internal IT projects, action will usually involve assessing the staff utilized on a project and reducing headcount or time spent. From the author's experience and research, the action step of project cost control is usually reactive, panicked, and unsystematic with many actions taken not preceded necessarily by an action impact assessment on the project. It is not expected that every little project action should be subjected to impact assessment, but all proposed key actions at least should undergo an impact assessment.

Challenges to Minimize for Effective Project Control in Practice

One of the principles of the PCIM project control methodology is that project control is not devolved from the environment in which it

Table 3.1 Challenges to minimize for effective project control in practice

Challenge categories	Identified project cost and time control issues
Organization	1. Lack of integration of cost and time during project control 2. Lack of senior management buy-in 3. Complicated project control systems and processes 4. Lack of a project control training regime
Project delivery approach	5. Lapses in integration of interfaces 6. Project control not being implemented from the early stages of a project 7. Inefficient utilization and control of human resources 8. Limited time devoted to planning how a project will be controlled at the outset
Client or owner issues	9. Excessive authorization gates 10. Use of adversarial and noncollaborative forms of contracts 11. Communication problems within client setup 12. Obstructive client representatives
Project team issues	13. Lack of detailed/complete design 14. Lack of trust among the project partners 15. Limited time devoted to project control on-site 16. Nonfactual reporting

operates. Therefore, there is a need to highlight the challenges of effective control of projects in practice and the provision of deeper insights into the day-to-day practical issues that make effective project cost and time control challenging from a practitioners' perspective. The research that underpinned the PCIM project control methodology unearthed many challenges to the achievement of effective project control in practice. These challenges have been grouped under four themes based on their origin during the project control process. The categories and issues are presented in Table 3.1 and the challenges and prevention are discussed in the remaining sections of this chapter.

Challenges Stemming From the Organization

Challenges stemming from the organization are the most important barrier to effective project controls. In fact, research by Munizaga and Olawale (2022) has found that many factors that engender project failure can be linked to organizational issues. This is because organizations may sometimes exhibit certain behaviors or lack certain practices that make effective project control more challenging. The project control challenges emanating from this category are discussed below.

Lack of Integration of Cost and Time During Project Control

This is a major obstacle to effective control of the cost and time objectives of projects. Project control in the "real sense" can only work if cost and time are integrated. However, this is not always the case in practice. Quite often in many organizations, there has been a little office with the planners (schedulers) in, there has been a little office with the cost or commercial people in, and never the two shall meet. This kind of situation should be avoided to achieve effective project cost and time control because lack of integration of time control with the cost dimension of the project would not yield the necessary information needed to act on a project effectively. To buttress the importance of integration of cost and time during project control, the classical research by Chan, Ho, and Tam (2001) also found that there is a strong relationship between cost and time of the projects. Additionally, this integration principle of cost and time has been exploited by Ballesteros-Pérez, Elamrousy, and González-Cruzc (2019) in developing time–cost trade-off models that help with fast-tracking the progress of projects.

Lack of Senior Management Buy-In

Senior management of some organizations often do not appreciate the benefits of a project control system and consequently do not give support to instituting a dedicated project control culture in the organization. Lack of senior management buy-in and absence of the right project control culture in an organization will often lead to project control being implemented half-heartedly with limited investment and training. Therefore, it is essential that management create a project control culture among all employees and provide all the support and encouragement needed. Research also supports this assertion; for example, it has been shown by Young and Poon (2013) that top management support is significantly more important for project success than any other factor. More specifically, Kanwal, Zafarb, and Bashira (2017) found from their research that top management support is important for project success, especially outcome control (or scope control) and cost and time control, that is, the classic "iron triangle" as discussed in Chapter 2.

Complicated Project Control Systems and Processes

Quite often, organizations put in place project control systems and processes that are complicated and end up being a bottleneck. They are sometimes considered burdensome and used half-heartedly. Consequently, the necessary information and data essential to achieve effective project control are often not up-to-date, inaccurate, or unavailable, leading to futility of project control efforts. Although implementation of projects is a relatively straightforward process, some systems overcomplicate its working, and the project management staff who use the systems do not like highly complicated systems. This is supported by the research by Bryde, Unterhitzenberger, and Jober (2018) who show that a small number of simple metrics and indices are more effective at communicating performance of projects than a large number and complicated ones.

Lack of Project Control Training Regime

This challenge relates strictly to the quality of training and knowledge that the people working on the project have about project control. Project control would be more effective if project delivery staff understood the science of project control better than they currently do. Research that underpins the PCIM project control methodology revealed that there is still a misconception that project control is just about Gantt charts as there is inadequate understanding of more robust project control techniques such as earned value analysis, progress analysis, S-curves, and so on. An organization that is serious about delivering projects effectively should not only put in place the necessary project control systems and processes but will also need to provide the necessary training needed to implement them correctly. Research by Bryde et al. (2018) has found that adequate training of all members of the project team, including contractors, is crucial for the smooth operation and use of project control systems.

Challenges Stemming From Project Delivery Approach

The importance of project delivery competence is buttressed by the PMI (2020), which found that 69 percent of organizations highly value project management but only 22 percent use standardized project management practices throughout their organization. Where the project management capability within an organization is not mature sufficiently to support the type of projects being delivered by or in the company, then project practitioners will find it challenging to deploy project controls successfully.

Lapses in Integration of Interfaces

One of the challenges of effective project controls is that practitioners often find it challenging to integrate the different interfaces of basic projects, let alone complex projects. The effect of this is that project control becomes a more difficult task. The numerous interfaces that often characterize many projects are not insurmountable, although the challenges they present cannot be underestimated. To mitigate this in practice, adequate planning is important as this is often lacking in the haste to start projects early. Adequate planning will reveal complex interfaces, therefore necessitating better preparation on how these interfaces will be controlled, as corroborated by Arrto, Ahola, and Vartiainen (2016) who found that integration is beneficial and creates value during the project delivery and has long-term value-enhancing impacts.

Project Control Not Being Implemented From the Early Stages of a Project

The project delivery team often does not pay much attention to the project progress and performance at the early stage, believing that there is still enough time to recover the project if progress stalls. However, as the project progresses, then the slippage can move from not being critical to becoming more critical or even moving to the critical path of the project (see Chapter 7 for information on CPM). Lack of attention from the very start of a project will subsequently lead to a frantic rush to finish the project through acceleration, which consequently impacts project control negatively and quite often increases the project cost. Therefore, it is important to always implement monitoring, reporting, and taking appropriate corrective actions right from the outset of a project, enabling potential project problems to be revealed earlier and controlled in an orderly and systematic manner.

Inefficient Utilization and Control of Human Resources

The efficient use of human resources is an important consideration in the successful delivery of projects. Therefore, eradicating unproductive use of labor is always of major importance in achieving effective cost and time control of projects. However, for example, in construction projects, the project delivery team on-site often finds it challenging to control the use of labor resources efficiently, which negatively affects the project control process. The research that informs the PCIM project control methodology revealed that labor utilization on projects is often not managed efficiently and sometimes not utilized as planned since most projects usually involve significant manhours, for example, digging and building in engineering, infrastructure, or pipeline projects, or coding and testing as in software development and IT projects. Not being proficient in the management of human resources will quite often have a detrimental impact on the effective control of the cost, time, and quality of the deliverables of a project.

Limited Time Devoted to Planning How a Project Will Be Controlled at the Outset

The project control approach to be adopted for a project needs to be planned at the outset of a project so that the project management team is aligned. Due to the varied level of experience of the project team members, alignment on project control approach is only achievable with the setting up of a set of project control guidelines at the outset. However, oftentimes how a project will be controlled before commencement of the project is not planned. This usually leads to an unstructured and non-systematic project control effort, which does not bode well for effective project control. The main reason for this is that, quite often, there is not enough lead time from when the contract to deliver a project is awarded to a contractor to when the contractor starts the project or for internally delivered projects, from when the approval to proceed is received from management to the project's start date. This leaves a very limited period for the project team and management to plan how the project will be controlled; it also hinders the installation of the necessary processes and systems that will ensure effective project control. The period between approval to proceed for internally delivered projects or tender receipt from external contractors and starting of work is very often "telescoped" and not sufficient. Consequently, many activities are rushed, leading to problems developing on the project. Research by Irfan, Khan, Hassan, Hassan, Habib, Khan, and Khan (2021) has found that preproject planning is important for the success of projects.

Challenges Stemming From the Client

When projects are being delivered to a client, some barriers to project control may emanate from the client processes and their approach to the project. Usually, this will relate to external clients, but it also covers projects delivered to business units or functions by their organization's project delivery team. To the project management team, the business unit is a client or customer.

Excessive Authorization Gates

A stage gate process is an aspect of project governance that enables decision makers to assess that a project is being delivered as planned. The stage gate process will provide an organizationwide approval process where the project team needs to seek authorization from members of an authorization board to progress a project from one stage to another or stop the project if certain criteria are not met (see Figure 3.3 for an example of a stage gate process from the author's experience). However, with everything, balance is important. If authorization gates are not proportionate to the value, pace, and complexity of projects being delivered, the project team's ability to make agile, tactical decisions may be restricted and become detrimental to effective project controls. The reason for this detrimental effect on project control is that, quite often, time is spent waiting for approval from a manager who may not be part of the project team and decisions that are by no means strategic cannot be made

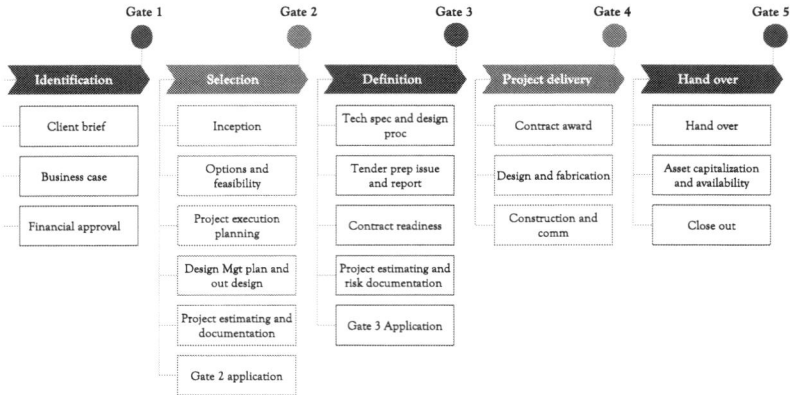

Figure 3.3 Example of a stage gate

by the project team. The authorization gate can then become a bottle-neck as it unnecessarily causes delay. While having authorization gates is a good management practice, too much authorization gates could lead to bureaucracy and inflexibility, which does not bode well for effective time and cost control.

Use of Adversarial and Noncollaborative Forms of Contracts

Projects usually involve interaction or use of other parties to execute the project. These relationships are usually guided by contracts. In process engineering projects, civil engineering projects, and building construction projects, for example, traditional standard forms of contracts like IChemE, ICE contract, and JCT contract are used, respectively. The form of contract adopted on projects helps in the allocation of risk and responsibilities to match the characteristics of different projects. However, contracts that are used on projects can either be collaborative or adversarial (where self-interest of the contracting parties mostly takes priority over everything, including their responsibilities on the project).

The use of adversarial types of contracts can often be a bottleneck during the project control process, as they do not aid openness and collaborative working and may sometimes prevent project partners from owning up to the mistakes that have been made. A classical empirical research by Larson (1995) asserts that "strictly adversarial" and even "guarded adversarial" contract approaches exhibited inferior project cost, time, and technical (scope) performance than those projects that employed a partnering approach. The challenge is most standard forms of contract used for a project have been traditionally adversarial; however, the project parties can overcome this challenge by having an ethos of openness and collaboration as part of their general project approach. There are now standard forms of contracts such as the standard forms of project partnering contracts and the NEC suite of contracts that have partnership and collaboration at their core.

Communication Problems Within Client Setup

Ineffective communication mostly within the client's organization often brings about conflicting information. Lack of clear and correct communication between a client's office staff and the project site representatives can sometimes lead to confusion. Inadequate or poor communication has also been identified by PMI (2018) as the primary cause of 29 percent of project failures. The research that informed the PCIM project control methodology also found that some client representatives communicate the changes they want without the client necessarily instructing it. This sometimes cause arguments, delay, and increased cost that the client later disputes. Research by Bryde et al. (2018) has found that high information asymmetry typically exists between project clients and contractors delivering the project, which needs to be addressed for project success. The importance of effective communication for effective project control cannot be overstated because project control relies on information and data. For effective project control to be achieved in practice, it is important that lines of communication are clear, and the most up-to-date information is communicated on time and to the relevant persons during the project control process.

Obstructive Client Representatives

Some client representatives can be obstructive in a bid to justify their importance and this does not create a team effort and a sleek project control process. According to the research underpinning the PCIM project control methodology, management problems with the client affecting project control quite often result from client representatives wanting to make sure that their position is safe by being overzealous to make sure that they've got a job. This kind of attitude from client representatives does not spell success for project control efforts and the project. To avoid this, it is imperative that all the project parties adopt a nonadversarial and collaborative approach for effective project control. In the author's experience of delivering projects and consulting on projects, the interaction between the client representative and the project management team is important in facilitating good project progress and budget performance through the selection of a client representative who can gain the confidence of the project team quickly. Additionally, client representatives on projects should understand that they have a fiduciary responsibility to the client. Fiduciary responsibility means acting on behalf of another person but in so doing putting the interest of the person you are acting far ahead of yours while in that capacity, with an ultimate responsibility to do so in good faith and trust.

Challenges Stemming From the Project Team

Since project delivery is a team effort with project control implementation relying on individual team members, some of the challenges to effective project control also stem from the project team.

Lack of Detailed or Complete Design

Most projects often must go through a design stage, be it designing a process plant, an infrastructure facility, or an IT system. However, the research that underpins this chapter revealed that for infrastructure and construction projects, for example, there has been a general decline in the production of detailed design, especially with the increased usage of the design and build procurement route. This sentiment would likely be reflected in other types of projects as well, especially with the increased pressure to get to market quickly, which has led to the development of, for example, new methods of delivery in IT, for example, Agile methodology. The real issue for the project delivery team is that the designs that are coming through for delivery and execution may not have the level of detail in them required for appropriate pricing or to do the job one-time, accurately and without the back-and-forth clarification with designers, which consequently causes delay, design/scope changes, and additional cost. Although it is not always possible to produce a detailed design for all projects, designing the project to as much detail as possible at the outset is bound to reduce resource and cost uncertainties associated with incomplete designs, thereby giving the project time, scope, and cost control effort a better chance of being effective. See Table 3.2 for case study of the negative implication of incomplete design on the cost and time objectives of a project.

Table 3.2 Real-life case study of the negative implication of incomplete design on the cost and time objective of a project

- The author was part of a consulting team that was engaged by the directors of a company, "Musicven group" for anonymity, that was developing an entertainment venue.
- The aim of the consultancy work was to carry out an independent review of the entertainment venue construction project to ascertain the reasons for the increase in the cost of the project.
- The overall cost of the entertainment arena had increased since the project was started. The cost increased by more than £6 million.
- The review carried out identified that the use of incomplete design was one of the primary causes of the cost overrun the project was facing, accounting for more than 40 % of the cost overrun.
- The review carried showed that Musicven group was under pressure for the entertainment venue to be ready by a set date. However, the assessment by Musicven group and their advisers concluded that there was not enough time to complete the full design of the entertainment venue, tender the project, appoint a contractor, and construct the entertainment arena before the set date.
- Therefore, the contractor tendering process and construction work had to begin before the building design was completed, resulting in the preliminary cost estimate and the tender to be based on an immature design.
- The consequence of this was that during the contractor tendering, the cost estimates for major aspects of the project were not accurate. As a result, when the design for the various aspects of the projects was completed during the project and then priced, their eventual cost showed a large increase than what was initially estimated.
- Additionally, because construction of the entertainment venue also started before the completion of design for some key areas, cost increases occurred due to the contractors waiting for the design and rework on some parts of the project that had been completed to accommodate the consequential effect of the completed design. An example was the heating, ventilation, and air conditioning services for the entertainment arena, which following the completion of design, had a price increase of more than 35%.
- Finally, in addition to the significant cost overrun encountered by the project, the project eventually encountered time overrun of more than 15 weeks, as a result of, waiting for the complete design of areas of the work that had not been designed and rework due to the impact of newly completed design.

Lack of Trust Among the Project Partners

In projects, there is usually a collection of participants all working together toward completion. So, some form of cooperation and trust is usually required from all parties to the project to complete the project even though they all try to protect their various interests. However, lack of trust often exists among the project team members. For example, it emerged from the PCIM methodology research that sometimes a project partner may try to hide a mistake from the rest of the project team in the hope that it can be rectified without the rest of the team knowing about it. This lack of transparency often leads to time and cost penalties of such errors not being analyzed on time. Any lack of transparency is bound to be problematic in the quest to achieve effective cost and time control, since information about the project cost and time performance is essential for the project control process. The importance of teamwork has been identified by the research of Oh, Lee, and Zo (2021) as important to project success. Trust has also been found by the research of Rezvani, Changa, Wiewioraa, Ashkanasy, Jordan, and Zolina (2016) as serving to enhance project success including in complex project situations.

Limited Time Devoted to Project Control On-Site

Projects are usually developed and delivered under time constraints and quite often the project delivery team members are not able to devote enough time to project control, as they are usually busy expending time and effort on core delivery activities. One reason for this is the impression that it will be very onerous to participate fully in the project control process and attention should be focused on completing the project, which can at times be frantic. Reports are therefore half-heartedly produced and rushed, usually not up-to-date and mostly inaccurate. The PCIM project control methodology research found that many members of the project delivery team are frequently of the opinion that they should be managing progress, delivering, or executing the project and they are usually under time pressure. Leading the project delivery team quite often means trying to focus on the issue at hand, and those leads might have been working overtime, leaving little time to report anything else. Consequentially, the data that is obtained from the project delivery team quite often isn't very good. The above sentiment that project control is an add-on to the duties involved in delivering a project can only be addressed by instilling a project control culture in an organization to the extent that the project management team, both on site and in the office, realize that project control is a good project management practice to be embraced by all.

Nonfactual Reporting

Reporting is a key step in project control, as it is how the status of the project in relation to the plan is communicated to the appropriate stakeholders including those with the responsibility to act should the project not be progressing as planned. The research that underpinned the PCIM project control methodology revealed that poor reporting is a common problem during project delivery and this problem needs to be dealt with for project control efforts to be effective. It was clear that reporting of information by the project delivery and sometimes management team is not always factual. One of the reasons for this is that project delivery personnel or even management are sometimes unwittingly optimistic about the status of the project or at worst dishonest to mask issues in the hope that they can bring a failing project back on track without raising the alarm to their senior staff based in the office. This problem has also been highlighted by the classical project reporting bias research by Snow, Keil, and Wallace (2007), which found that project managers produce biased reports 60 percent of the time and the bias is more than twice as likely to be optimistic than pessimistic. Consequently, the reported information, which is used during the analysis stage of project control, ultimately produces results that will not give a true reflection of the project. Therefore, areas needing corrective action will not be obvious to senior managers, making time and cost control ineffective. To give project control a better chance of success, it is important that reports are factual, true, and accurate. This will enable the information in the reports to highlight the true project progress, scope, and time status so that actions can be taken to bring the project back on track if necessary. See Table 3.3 for case study of nonfactual reporting.

Table 3.3 Real-life case study of nonfactual reporting:
Crossrail mega project

Introduction
The author was part of the consulting team that was appointed by the project sponsors,
Transport for London (TfL) and the UK Department for Transport (DfT), in October
2018 to carry out independent financial, commercial, and governance reviews of
the Crossrail mega project following the sudden announcement that the project had
encountered delay and cost overrun. Commercial reporting and oversight were one of
the many areas that the project sponsors wanted the team of consultants to review.

Background
London's Crossrail was planned as a £15 billion mega project to provide a new
cross-London rail service, running through a newly constructed section beneath central
London, including new rail tunnels and underground stations. The project was meant
to be completed and opened for operations in December 2018. However, in August
2018, the project developer, Crossrail Limited, announced that the project could not be
completed and opened for operations on the planned date and will be delayed for more
than nine months! (It was eventually delayed for three and half years). Additionally,
it emerged that the £15 billion would not be enough to complete the project and the
project requested an additional funding of £2 billion! The fact that the project will be
delayed and that it will encounter cost overrun of such magnitude came as a surprise to
the sponsors and stakeholders because up until that point all the reports issued by the
project had maintained that it was on track to be opened by December 2018. Surely, a
delay of more than nine months and additional funding requirements of that magnitude
did not just appear to the project management team four months before their reported
opening date.

Findings in relation to reporting
The author and his team found, among other things, that factual reporting had not been
happening on the project for a long time. It was found that the project's performance
monitoring and reporting has not led to timely and adequate advance notice being provided on the need to materially change the opening date and the resulting significant
cost impact. Although there was reporting flow from the project teams to management
and the project leadership/board and to the sponsors, "the resultant reporting within
and by the project was neither sufficiently timely nor sufficiently clear as to the impacts
and magnitude of the range of probable consequences of the issues within the project"
(KPMG's independent review of Crossrail report 2019). In essence, the warning signs
of the delay and cost overrun had been there at least 12 months prior to the announcement and that most project staff on the project knew that the December 2018 opening
date was not realistic, especially as some key parts of the project did not start when they
should have started. For example, the dynamic train testing should have started in early
2018, but it did not and that would have made it very clear that the project would be
delayed. However, because the project had been successful in the early stages and had
built a reputation of being a model project, the leadership team of the project wanted
to hold on to this reputation and continued to report that the project was on-time and
on-budget. Despite the signs showing otherwise in the hope that they could recover the
situation, they did not report externally the challenges being faced long beyond when
they should have done.

Summary

Project control is important in preventing project failure. However, achieving effective project control in practice is often challenging. The challenges to achieving effective cost and time control of construction projects in practice as well as recommendations to address these have been described. Sixteen key challenges were identified with many submissions put forward to address them. These are classified into four categories based on their origin as follows: (1) from the organization; (2) from the project delivery approach; (3) from the client; and (4) from the project team. It was recommended that cost and time control should also always be integrated, since controlling one without the other is unlikely to be effective. Factual and accurate reporting was also seen as important in avoiding some of these challenges.

Adequate planning was put forward to ensuring better preparation on how complex interfaces will be controlled on projects. Similarly, it was recommended that project control systems and processes should always be in place before rushing to commence a project. However, it was highlighted that authorization gates should be proportionate to the type of projects so that they don't lead to unnecessary bottlenecks in the project control process. Finally, the importance of good communication for effective project cost and time control was stressed since it is essential that lines of communication are clear and the most up-to-date and accurate information is communicated on time and to the relevant persons during the project control process. Being aware of these challenges will help project control practitioners and organizations as they will be able to guard against them during the project control effort leading to the achievement of improved project controls.

CHAPTER 4

Using the Project Control Inhibitors Management (PCIM) Methodology to Improve Project Control in Practice

Improving the Project Control in Practice

Researchers all through the years have proposed new approaches that can be used to improve project control. However, most of these research have been focused on individual areas of project control such as techniques, causes of project cost and time overrun, and project success factors. A literature review carried out during the PCIM project control methodology research revealed that there is a dearth of comprehensive research on the improvement of the project control process in its entirety. Viewing project control as just about the use of a technique or a software tool is an incomplete approach because project control encompasses the techniques, software tools use, practices, and the environment where project control is taking place. The deficiency of a comprehensive approach to project controls is one of the reasons the research that informed the PCIM project control methodology was carried out.

The PCIM Methodology

Many of the project control methodologies in existence only describe what, not how effective, project control should be implemented. Although several studies describe what an ideal project control process should look like diagrammatically, mathematically, or the isolation of a project management control success factor, there is not much that has been written on how they can be utilized in practice.

Second, and most importantly, many of the studies that have informed the development of these approaches are not well grounded in project control practice. As most of the developed approaches have not involved practitioners in their development. Therefore, it is questionable how accurately they reflect the real problems faced by project management practitioners during the project control practice. These conclusions underlie the need for an improved project cost and time control approach and the rationale for research that underpin the development of the PCIM project control methodology.

The development of the PCIM project control methodology focused on classical triple constraints of projects (cost, scope, and time) and adopted a collaborative and contingent (situational) approach through the involvement of practitioners to draw out their needs, requirements, bottlenecks, and current issues in practice.

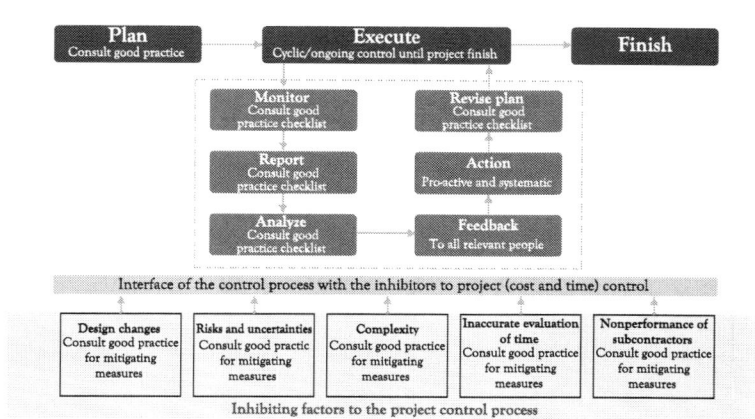

Figure 4.1 PCIM methodology framework

The PCIM project control methodology is focused on three primary areas during project control:

i. The project phases, that is, plan, execute, and deliver and finish;
ii. The project control steps; and
iii. Factors that inhibit effective project control.

The PCIM approach is depicted in Figure 4.1. The top section covers the primary phases through which a project proceeds (plan, execute, and finish), the middle section includes the primary project control steps (monitor, report, analyze, feedback, action, and revise plan), and the bottom section reflects the fact that project control is not a closed system and is often inhibited by some factors. The leading project control inhibitors from the research conducted in the construction and infrastructure project industry in the UK include design changes, risks and uncertainties, complexity, inaccurate evaluation of time, and nonperformance of subcontractors. This framework includes two sets of good practice checklists, which provide advice on the project control process. One set contained numerous mitigating good practices for the leading project cost and time control inhibitor (see Chapter 5). The second set contained several good practices for the major steps of the control cycle (planning, monitoring, reporting, and analyzing (see Chapter 6)). The processes of the PCIM project control methodology are described in the following sections.

Plan the Project Control Process

The PCIM methodology recommends that project control should start at the planning stage of a project. The reason for this is that quite often project management practitioners do not plan how a project will be controlled at the outset of the project. During the planning stage of the project, much effort is often spent on planning how the project will be executed. For example, various types of schedule of works are used to sequence the activities to be performed. Detailed cost estimates and cost plans are also produced. However, these plans are often developed without giving prior thought to how they will be used for project control. Similar to the assertion of Fewings and Henjewele (2019) who stated that the control system is critical to the health of the project, and its choice should influence the planning process rather than vice versa.

The PCIM methodology identifies this problem and recommends that during the planning stage of a project, in addition to production of the schedule of works and cost estimates, consideration should be given to how the project will be controlled during the execution stage. Therefore, a very important component of the PCIM project control methodology is the preparation of a document during the planning phase of the project that details how the project will be controlled. This document has been termed the project control implementation document (PCID). The document will set out the following:

- Project control tools and techniques to be used during the project;
- Frequency of monitoring and reporting;
- Destination of the reports;
- Templates of the reports;
- Duties of the project team as it relates to controlling the project;
- Other information deemed necessary for effective control.

The PCID should be prepared by the project manager in consultation with the other members of the project team, and it should be circulated to the entire project team, including project team members working in external project sites. The PCID for each project should be reviewed regularly by the project manager to ascertain that the project is being controlled as planned.

Execute

The PCIM methodology moves from planning to the execution phase of the project. The execution phase of a project is the phase in which the plan is put into practice to bring the concept into reality. It is during this stage that control of cost and time is primarily needed because it is the riskiest phase of the project; things can often go wrong, and the plan developed at the outset is tested. Project control during this phase consists of a cyclic and iterative process of the following activities.

Monitoring

After the project has been planned and the plan put into execution, this original plan needs to be monitored during the execution stage. Monitoring is the process of observing systematically the position of the project all through the course of delivering the project and documenting the information obtained so that the performance of the project can be revealed. It aims to determine whether the intended objectives have been met.

The monitoring step of the PCIM project control methodology, first, suggests that monitoring should be a distinct step in the control cycle as opposed to the prevalent practice, in which monitoring is barely done by the project delivery team (see Chapter 3), and control seems to move straight from planning to reporting by project-based cost experts such as quantity surveyor for construction projects or cost engineer in process engineering projects. Although having project-based cost experts like this is not being discounted and can provide good reports, it will be better if, in addition to reporting, monitoring is incorporated into the practices or duties of the delivery team on the project site.

Reporting

The next step of the PCIM project control methodology is reporting. Reporting provides a straightforward statement of the work accomplished, predicts future accomplishment in terms of the project's scope, cost, and schedule, and measures actual accomplishments against goals set forth in the plan. It reveals the problems in the project and potential risk areas so that management can act to stop or minimize these problems and risks.

In practice, although the research underpinning the PCIM methodology found that cost control reporting seems robust in practice, given that it is often performed by a project-based cost team member, the reporting on time control is at best loose (see Chapter 3). The PCIM approach advocates a more structured process through, for example, incorporation of the reporting regime for the project in the PCID at the project outset. This will specify the reporting templates, reporting cycle, destination of reports, and ensures that reporting is not solely achieved through progress meetings but is instead systematic and regular. Simple software packages should also be used to aid reporting and allow reports to be sent to the departments responsible for collating and analyzing these reports.

The PCIM approach also proposes that time and cost reporting should be conducted together rather than separately. This can be achieved through the use of reporting templates that contain both cost and time information to aid the integration of cost and time control. This will combat the prevailing practice in which management of time is left to the planning department, management of the cost estimate/cost plan is left to another department such as cost management or project accounting, and the two rarely report jointly.

Analysis

From reporting, next in the PCIM framework is the analyzing step, during which cost, and time information contained in the submitted report is analyzed. This is the step where the team needs to assess whether the project is performing as desired and compute the extent of variance. This is one of the most important steps during the control process because, if performed properly, the analysis step could go a long way in improving a failing project.

The problem with the analysis step in practice is that the full potential of analysis is not explored. The analysis step is more of interpretation of the information reported instead of analysis. The prevailing practice as found by the research underpinning the PCIM methodology, is that analysis often does not integrate cost, scope, and time during this important step. This is usually not an effective approach since classical research by Jung and Woo (2004) has highlighted the fact that cost and scheduling are closely interrelated, because cost and time share a lot of common data in their controlling processes on projects. Therefore, integrating cost and schedule control functions provides an effective tool for monitoring cost and time performance during the execution process of a project.

Not integrating cost and time analysis will invariably generate results that are not very useful for the next step of the control process because any action to bring the project back on track, for example, will usually have a cost implication. The PCIM project control methodology avoids these shortcomings by advocating that techniques that combine cost and time data are used during analysis to foster the integration of cost, scope, and time controls. Additionally, the approach goes beyond just interpretation but advocates trending and the use of the results to forecast the future performance of a project. A useful technique that can be used to achieve this is the earned value analysis and management (see Chapter 8). The earned value method is very effective for most projects and provides the added benefit of utilizing cost, scope, and time information. It considers the work completed, the time taken, and the costs incurred to complete the project. This provides results that are useful for both the cost, scope, and time objectives of the project, thereby allowing integration of both cost and time.

Feedback

From the analysis step, the PCIM project control methodology advocates a dedicated feedback action. Feedback is the process of disseminating the results of the analysis conducted on the information from the monitoring and reporting steps to all the necessary participants and relevant stakeholders involved in the project. This is very important during the project control process, but interestingly, quite often, this is not reinforced in most project control models. According to the PCIM project control methodology research, feedback was also found to be missing from the prevailing cost and time control process in practice as explained in the previous chapter, where it was revealed that in practice, there is usually no systematic method of disseminating the findings of the analysis step. What normally happens is that if analysis reveals that action(s) are required to bring the project back on track, quite often, at best, only ad hoc meetings are held to discuss the situation. The results of the analysis step need to be transmitted to everybody who has an action to take; otherwise, the effort that has been put into collecting information, reporting, and analyzing will be in vain.

The PCIM project control methodology stresses that, irrespective of the results of the analysis, systems and processes should be put in place to provide feedback on the findings to the project delivery team. In practice, transfer of project control information is often only one way, that is, from the delivery team to the project office. The project office rarely provides feedback on their findings to the project delivery team on-site except for when the findings are negative.

The PCIM project control methodology suggests the use of a feedback report from the project control team sent at set periods to the project delivery site team. This will go a long way in motivating them that the monitoring and reporting they conduct and transmit to the project office is not useless information but is being used. This will also instill a project control culture in the organization. This feedback report should also be sent to senior managers, and the project decision makers who can act on the findings of the analysis stage. Finally, having a dedicated feedback procedure ensures that information is transmitted quickly and efficiently and is not left on the desk until it becomes obsolete and useless.

Action

The action step ensures that information revealed from the analysis step is put into practice. To close the control loop, the team must take effective action to overcome any variances. This involves identifying and evaluating alternative courses of action for resolving a perceived problem situation. Corrective or mitigating actions need to be timely, practical, and should be consistent with the project objectives and plan.

The PCIM project control methodology specifically reinforces the need for actions not only to be reactive but primarily proactive. In the prevailing project control process used in practice, action is primarily reactive. In other words, action is only taken to correct things that have gone wrong. Reactive actions are often not effective during project control; hence, the PCIM methodology advocates that action should be reactive and proactive. Information generated during analysis should be able to highlight possible problems and develop remedial actions well in advance instead of waiting for problems to occur or, even worse, after they have occurred (as is often the case in practice as detailed in Chapter 3); action should always be taken immediately if possible.

The PCIM project control methodology also recommends that the process of implementing remedial actions during project control should not be haphazard; instead, it should be controlled and systematic. Acting systematically would, for example, involves conducting an impact analysis on the action that will be taken before acting. Some actions may create risks and problems in the future; some actions may cause delays to the project, incur cost increases, or raise quality issues. Therefore, it is important that both the time and cost implications of planned corrective or mitigating actions are analyzed fully and appreciated by appropriate project parties and stakeholders as soon as possible. If actions are not systematic, not all the members of the project team will be aware of the action and this will be counterproductive. Therefore, a systematic approach is essential when deciding on the best course of action to get a project back on track during project control. Finally, all the relevant people that will be involved in and impacted by a remedial action should be notified and informed of their involvement. Additionally, the project team and stakeholders should together plan (not planning in isolation) how the action will be implemented, so that any consequential effect to other areas of the project can be identified.

Revise Plan

The PCIM framework moves from action into the revised plan. Revision of a plan involves the updating of the previous project plan to reflect the impact of any action taken because of the analysis conducted on the project. This has been treated as a separate step instead of tagging it to the original planning step (as often the case in practice) because the PCIM project control approach recognizes that this is a process that requires due diligence.

The research underpinning the development of the PCIM project control methodology revealed that, in practice, when action is taken, the status quo often resumes, and revisions of the project schedule are produced by just being updated with the action that has already been taken or updating the cost plan and budget (see Chapter 3). The revise plan step in the PCIM project control framework goes beyond just updating the old project plan. This is because the actions that are taken will often exert an impact on the remaining activities of the project. Therefore, revision of the schedule and cost plan needs to be more rigorous than just updating. The initial plan should always be kept as a baseline, whereas the revised plan should be used for continuing the project. Revised plan marks the end of one iteration of a cyclic and iterative process, which should be repeated continuously while the project is still being executed.

Finish

Finally, the PCIM project control methodology framework moves to the finish step. This is when the project has been completed and the original conceived plan or an iteratively revised plan accepted by all parties during the project has been achieved. At this point of the project, the PCIM methodology supports the carrying out of a formal project lesson learned session (not long after completing the project) by all members of the project team, especially in relation to the effectiveness of the project control regime implemented on the project. This will serve as a feedback to improve the overall project control process and practice within the organization.

Project Control Inhibitors

The next section of the PCIM framework shows the inhibitors to the cost and time control process. This is because project control techniques are often recommended without additional suggestions in relation to the enabling environment required for their success. The research that informed the PCIM project control methodology identified inhibitors to effective project cost and time control in the UK construction and infrastructure industry (see Chapter 5 for more details). The research revealed that the leading five factors that inhibited time control are also the leading five inhibitors of cost control. This goes with the saying "time is money"; in the author's experience of working on projects, many reasons for cost increases relate to schedule and vice versa. The leading five project cost and time control inhibitors identified are design and scope changes, risk and uncertainty, inaccurate evaluation of project time duration, complexity of works, and nonperformance of subcontractors.

The PCIM Project Control Methodology Good Practice Checklist

The final ingredient of the PCIM project control methodology is a checklist of good practices. Deliberate documentation and implementation of good practices within the organization are important because it will facilitate the development of a project control culture through embedding of these good practices in an organization. And alongside this, it will enhance staff competency and organizational capability through training on the use of these good practices and enable continuous improvement. Therefore, modeling the project control steps is only half the story of the control process in practice because any developed project control framework still depends on people to put it into use. One of the problems of project control in practice is that many project managers often lack a sense of direction and guidance of what to do. Therefore, the research underpinning the development of the PCIM project control methodology developed two sets of good practices checklist. First, a set of good practice checklist was developed for the five leading project control inhibitors discussed in the previous section because of their importance to effective project control, and to help mitigate their negative impact on project cost and time control. Second, another set of good practices was developed for the major steps of the control process (plan, monitor, report, and analyze) because they form the crux of the project control process.

The developed good practice checklists are an integral component of the PCIM project control methodology and provide guidance to users. These good practice checklists are presented and discussed in detail in Chapters 5 and 6. These good practice checklists are by no means exhaustive. Companies and individual practitioners can add additional good practices to the existing checklists or create new checklists for other project control inhibitors, which might be particularly important to them. The primary purpose of these checklists is to act as a starting point for practitioners to use during the project cost, scope, and time control process.

Scalability of the PCIM Project Control Methodology

The process used in the development of the PCIM project control methodology can also be used as a blueprint for developing a control process specific to a project. For example, the framework used for the development of the PCIM methodology can be used in the development of a more specific control model for any desired type of project such as IT projects, process engineering projects, pharmaceutical research and development projects, and so on. It can also be used in developing control models to be used by serial clients for the type of projects they invest in or the area of the project life cycle they are most active. For example, a client might adapt the PCIM approach using the framework in this study just for the preconstruction phase of its design and build projects since that is mostly where its risk lies and not the construction phase.

Another way the PCIM project control approach that can be used as a blueprint is in developing project controls specific to the environment in which a project is being executed. The reason for this is that the project control inhibitors that have been incorporated as part of the PCIM project control methodology were brought to light based on a research conducted in a developed economy. These factors may be different from the pressing factors in a developing country, for example, where the inhibitors to the cost and time control effort may be different from those in a developed economy. Therefore, the framework used for the identification of these factors and the development of mitigating measures may be used to identify inhibitors and their mitigations as specific to projects being implemented in any type of macroeconomic environment or country if so desired. It is important to note that the good practices developed for the project control cycle will be the same irrespective of the type of project or the location country where the project is taking place.

Barriers to the Implementing the PCIM Methodology

It is important to highlight some of the barriers that may be faced in implementing the PCIM project control approach.

Organizational Cultural Change

First, cultural change may be a key barrier to implementing the PCIM project control methodology successfully because one of its important requirements is the need to get cost and scheduling professionals to work together. However, the culture in projects, especially infrastructure projects as noted in chapter three, is that these are separate disciplines and getting them to work together will require a dedicated effort by management. This may involve some organizational restructuring and the inconvenience of doing this may be seen to outweigh the perceived benefits.

This barrier may easily be surmounted because the PCIM project control approach has combined the two structures (scheduling and cost) that are mostly separated but are dependent on each other. Therefore, the management will need to work at convincing these two disciplines that utilizing the PCIM approach for project control and working together will eliminate duplication of effort. The implication of this is that implementing the PCIM project control approach may be difficult at first, but the benefit will soon become obvious as time goes on.

Cost Implications of Change

Another potential barrier is the perceived cost implication of modifying existing systems, for example, modifying software packages, reporting templates, training in the use of new techniques, and so on may be considered costly. But this can be prevented by stressing to the senior management that the PCIM project control methodology is not advocating a total departure from the tangible aspects of project control in practice, what it does is bring a focused structure to the process of project control in practice. For example, some of the techniques like the earned value analysis and CPM advocated in the PCIM project control methodology are techniques that are already in existence and used in practice. What is needed is training in the use of these techniques and management support to see that the process advocated by the PCIM project control methodology is followed. There may also be a demand for additional compensation by staff due to a perceived addition to their responsibilities; this will be overcome by highlighting that the process will make their job easier.

Management Buy-In

Another potential barrier to the implementation of the PCIM project control methodology is that it depends on management buy-in because as metioned previously, the PCIM project control methodology requires, for example, a cultural change, realignment of existing processes and so on as these changes will never happen if there is no management buy-in. If the senior management of a company does not support the utilization of the PCIM project control methodology and the requirements needed to implement it, then its use will falter as soon as implementation begins. Therefore, to prevent this from happening, it is essential that management instills in the psyche of all employees the need to utilize the PCIM project control approach and accompanying good practice checklist and follow the recommended steps. Management should also provide all the support and encouragement needed to make it work to realize the full benefits of implementing the PCIM methodology and for it to stand the test of time.

It is also important to point out that the PCIM project control methodology is not intended to be a "silver bullet." The PCIM project control approach, especially the incorporation of the project control inhibitors, their mitigating good practices, and good practice checklist for the cyclical project control steps, should be a minimum requirement for the project control process.

Case Study: Practical Value of the PCIM Project Control Methodology

The practical applicability of the PCIM project control methodology and its potential benefits can be illustrated using a real-world example of a construction company, for which the author had worked as a project manager. The firm, "Constructwell Ltd" for anonymity, is involved in projects, which usually last between 3 and 12 months. It employed project managers with varied levels of experience. Each project manager usually handled up to four projects simultaneously depending on project size and complexity.

Although Constructwell Ltd. had an established accounting and financial control system and an ISO-certified quality control system in place, it had no standard project control methods. Each project manager adopted ad hoc procedures and decided the type and detail of the schedule at his/her own discretion. In addition, although most of the project managers were trained to an appropriate level, rendering them aware of project control techniques such as EVM, CPM, and S-curves. These techniques were not used in the analysis of project progress because of a lack of standardized project control process within the organization. Furthermore, when remedial actions were required, they were usually decided based on the experience of the individual project managers rather than on any systematic approach. As a result, delays and cost overruns were common in many projects of Constructwell Ltd.

The PCIM project control methodology would be beneficial to Constructwell Ltd. in several ways as described below:

- The PCIM project control methodology requires a project team to develop a project control implementation document (PCID) at the outset of the project.
- This will help to impose a standardized project control procedure and will provide a basis for measuring and improving performance of project controls.
- Adopting the PCIM methodology would promote proactive culture toward project control in Constructwell Ltd. Project managers will follow a clear process to monitor, review, and manage variations of cost, scope, and time during projects. The use of the good practice checklists and integrated reporting templates will further formalize project control practice throughout the entire company.
- The normal practice of project progress analysis at Constructwell Ltd. was through a qualitative evaluation of the reported progress against the planned progress and by assessment of subcontractor's invoices in relation to the work package cost budget. Cost and time were often assessed separately; holistic assessment was difficult.
- The PCIM project control method addresses this issue by always advocating integrated quantitative analysis of cost and time information.
- The dedicated feedback phase of the PCIM approach will ensure that the results of analysis are fed back immediately to the project manager and other team members from whom actions are required. This will lead to prompt actions and

timely update of cost and schedule information, avoiding the current situation in which schedule of works is updated regularly, but cost plan is only revised later for final accounts purposes.

- The PCIM project control methodology requires an impact analysis to be conducted on all potential corrective actions by evaluating the potential domino effect of any action and the feasibility of its implementation. This will help project managers to choose the optimum solution rather than the first solution that comes to mind.

- Use of the PCIM project control methodology, especially the good practice checklists, will remove the lack of a sense of direction and guidance of project managers on good practices to adopt during project control. These checklists will be reviewed periodically to ensure their applicability to the types of projects and project stages at Constructwell Ltd.

CHAPTER 5

Good Practices to Mitigate the Foremost Project Cost and Time Control Inhibitors

The Need for a Checklist of Good Practices During Project Control

As discussed in Chapter 4, the project control inhibitors management (PCIM) methodology argues that it is not good enough to have developed a process for use in an organization without building it into the practices that will enable success. The underlying hypothesis of the PCIM methodology is that to control a project successfully, it is important to recognize that you need to identify and manage the factors that inhibit project managers from effectively controlling the project.

The PCIM methodology also asserts that it is important to note that the project control process is not a closed system and is often affected by many factors including inhibitors. This is because projects are affected by their internal and external environment so the control effort being expended on a project by practitioners in practice is also affected by some issues that may inhibit the effectiveness of the control effort. Hence why many projects still encounter cost and time overrun despite the application of controls to the cost and time objectives of projects. Therefore, this important hypothesis (existence of project control inhibitors), which is often missing from most project control models, is incorporated in the PCIM project control methodology. The PCIM project control methodology then recommends that any developed project control approach should incorporate practices, or mitigating measures, that can be used to combat these project control inhibitors. This unique attribute proposed by the PCIM methodology is discussed in the next sections. The good practices of the PCIM presented in this chapter have emanated from the construction/infrastructure project sector. However, from the author's experience of working on projects across many industries, majority of these good practices are applicable to projects in other industries, especially as the developed good practices cover project management issues and not technical industry factors.

Most Common Project Control Inhibitors and Classification of Their Mitigating Measures

The research that informed the PCIM project control methodology identified more than 60 factors that could inhibit the effective control of project cost, scope, and time by conducting a detailed analysis of research literature in this area. However, some of these factors were found to overlap or related to each other, therefore necessitating further analysis such as merging, elimination of similar factors, and so on. Following this analysis, 20 factors that can potentially inhibit effective project cost, scope, and time control were shortlisted for further research aimed at prioritizing them in order of how frequently they inhibit the project control process. Prior to this, the 20 project control inhibitors (see Table 5.1) are classified according to the source of these factors as: (1) exogenous factors; (2) endogenous organizational factors; and (3) endogenous project internal factors. These are discussed in the following three subsections.

Exogenous Inhibitors

These project control inhibitors are factors that stem from outside the project environment; these are mostly macroeconomic factors and sociopolitical factors but could also be natural factors. The project control inhibitors that were identified as making up this group as presented in Table 5.1 include economic factors like unstable interest rate, inflation of prices, and fluctuation of currency. Other factors in this group include sociopolitical factors such as unstable government policies, weak regulatory regime, and dependency on imported materials. Although these project control inhibitors are not related directly to the project, they can affect the ability to control cost, scope, and time of construction projects. For example, projects normally utilize numerous types of materials that

Table 5.1 Classification of the identified project cost and time control inhibitors

Project cost and time control inhibitors	
Exogenous factors	
A	Unstable interest rate
B	Dependency on imported materials
C	Inflation of prices
D	Fluctuation of currency/exchange rate
E	Unstable government policies
F	Weak regulation and control
G	Unpredictable weather conditions
Endogenous organizational factors	
H	Low skilled manpower
I	Lack of proper training and experience of project management
J	Lack of appropriate software
Endogenous project-based factors	
K	Inaccurate evaluation of projects time/duration
L	Project fraud and corruption
M	Design and scope changes
N	Financing and payment for completed works
O	Complexity of works
P	Discrepancies in contract documentation
Q	Contract and specification interpretation disagreement
R	Conflict between project parties
S	Risk and uncertainty associated with projects

will need to be procured but if there is high inflation, the cost of materials may be affected and ultimately the planned and outturn cost of a project. Similarly, if weather conditions turned out worse than had been envisaged, they may affect the ability to control the time and scope of a project effectively and ultimately the cost.

Endogenous Organizational Inhibitors

This category contains project inhibitors that are related to the project than the external environment factors. These project control inhibitors would not normally stem from implementing the project, rather they stem from the project office or decisions made by the organization in relation to the project. For example, if an inexperienced project manager is assigned to manage a project, this weakness does not stem from the project; it is a project office deficiency or, if there is a lack of an appropriate project control software that can be used for the project, this may inhibit the ability to control time in a project effectively.

Endogenous Project-Based Inhibitors

These are project control inhibitors that stem directly from implementing the project. Some of the factors in this category include nonperformance of subcontractors, scope and design changes, conflict between project parties, inaccurate evaluation of project time/duration, and so on. They can originate from any of the project parties; for example, scope and design changes can be requested by the client or the client representative in a traditional procurement approach in which the project has been designed fully by the client representatives before being given to contractors to execute, or requested by the contractor in a design and build procurement approach. They can also come prior to the start of executing a project such as discrepancy in contract documentation, inaccurate evaluation of time, or during execution. These project control inhibitors can also continue to affect the project negatively even after execution or delivery adding to the final project cost, for example, conflict between project parties, which could lead to cost of adjudication, arbitration, or litigation.

Leading Project (Cost and Time) Control Inhibitors

Further analysis (using the relative importance index (RII) technique) was carried out as part of the PCIM methodology research to prioritize these 20 project control inhibitors in order of how common they are at inhibiting effective project cost and time control (see Table 5.2).

The RII data analysis technique was used to determine the relative importance of the project control inhibitors as rated by the construction project practitioners during the PCIM project control methodology research. To enable the use of the RII technique, the questionnaire utilized

Table 5.2 Ranking of inhibitors to effective project time and cost control

Project control inhibitors	Time control		Cost control	
	RII	Rank	RII	Rank
Design and scope changes	0.94	1	0.94	1
Inaccurate evaluation of projects time/duration	0.86	2	0.86	3
Complexity of works	0.86	3	0.81	5
Risk and uncertainty associated with projects	0.85	4	0.89	2
Nonperformance of subcontractors and nominated suppliers	0.85	5	0.82	4
Lack of proper training and experience of project manager	0.78	6	0.77	11
Discrepancies in contract documentation	0.77	7	0.80	7
Low skilled manpower	0.74	8	0.69	12
Conflict between project parties	0.74	9	0.81	6
Unpredictable weather conditions	0.74	10	0.68	13
Financing and payment for completed works	0.73	11	0.78	10
Contract and specification interpretation disagreement	0.71	12	0.80	8
Dependency on imported materials	0.66	13	0.65	14
Lack of appropriate software	0.61	14	0.62	15
Inflation of prices	0.58	15	0.79	9
Weak regulation and control	0.55	16	0.58	18
Project fraud and corruption	0.50	17	0.55	19
Unstable government policies	0.47	18	0.48	20
Unstable interest rate	0.46	19	0.59	16
Fluctuation of currency/exchange rate	0.45	20	0.58	17

a four-point scale for the rating by practitioners. A numerical value was assigned to the ratings available for each of the project control inhibitor as follows: 4, extremely important; 3, important; 2, unimportant; 1, extremely unimportant. This four-point scale was converted to a RII for each of the project control inhibitors using the following equation:

$$\text{Relative importance index (RII)} = \sum W \div (H \times N)$$

where:

- W is the weight given to each project control inhibitor by the practitioners, which ranges from one to four. Therefore, $\sum W$ is calculated by addition of the various weightings given to a project control inhibitor by all the practitioners.
- H is the highest rating available (that is 4, "very important").
- N is the total number of practitioners who have answered the question.

In a case where two or more project control inhibitors obtained the same RII, the determination of the ranking was based on the project control inhibitor that got more "very important" rating.

The RII analysis revealed that the top five project cost and time control inhibitors (in order of importance) in construction and infrastructure projects in the UK are:

1. Design and scope changes
2. Risks and uncertainties
3. Inaccurate evaluation of project time/duration
4. Complexity of works
5. Nonperformance of subcontractors

From Table 5.2, the top five inhibitors to effective time control are also the leading inhibitors to effective cost control, albeit in slightly different order. Topping the list for both cost and time control is design and scope changes. Design and scope change is undoubtedly considered the most important factor that affects the ability to control cost and time of projects. This is no surprise because scope is one of the triple constraints of projects, which is also called the classical "iron triangle" of project management (see chapter 2). Therefore, design and scope changes will normally have a cost and time implication. If the process of design and scope change is not well managed, it will undoubtedly affect the progress (time) as well as the cost of the project negatively. Frequent and haphazard design and scope change requests during a project can often be a major bottleneck to effective control. Risk and uncertainty was the next leading project cost and time control inhibitor. This is no surprise because projects are affected by uncertainties and risks and if a risk to a project comes to fruition, the impact is usually increased cost and/or delay to the project. Therefore, if risks and uncertainties are not dealt with effectively on projects, controlling cost and time will be a great challenge.

Another leading project control inhibitor is inaccurate evaluation of project time/duration. It's no surprise that this is considered a critical time and cost control inhibitor because if the time duration of projects is not accurate, then time control is already a lost cause. It then becomes impossible to control effectively the time of projects and consequentially the cost, because if the work goes on for longer than planned, then it will lead to more resources being expended on the project, ultimately affecting the cost as well. The complexity of works during project delivery was also found by the PCIM project control methodology research as a leading cost and time control inhibitor. This is because the more complex a project is, the more challenging it will be to know for certain the cost and time due to unknown challenges that may emerge during delivery, which would usually affect cost and time duration. The fifth ranked leading project control inhibitor, nonperformance of subcontractors and suppliers, is important because many projects usually rely on or involve subcontractors or suppliers during their delivery. When subcontractors and suppliers are not reliable, for example, delaying project materials or not completing work on time, then the control of cost and time will be a challenge.

Similarities Between Project Cost Control Inhibitors and Project Time Control Inhibitors

The research that underpinned the PCIM project control methodology found a strong positive correlation between the ranking of time control inhibitors and cost control inhibitors. This corroborates a classical research in this area by Chang (2002), which found that it is difficult to separate the reasons causing overrun into that of cost and schedule, because many reasons for time extensions are normally also the reasons for cost increases. Therefore, it can be asserted that the factors that inhibit effective time control of projects are also likely to inhibit effective cost control.

In addition to the top five project control inhibitors being the same for both cost and time control, the factors that were ranked lowest are also all similar for cost and time control. The five lowest ranked factors for time control are: weak regulation and control; project fraud and corruption; unstable government policies; unstable interest rate; and fluctuation of currency/exchange rates.

In addition to the fact that the leading five project cost and time control inhibitors are similar, with very similar RII, they are also endogenous project factors using the classification system in Table 5.1 earlier. This shows that the factors that mostly inhibit effective project cost and time control are those that stem from the project. This may seem worrying on the face of it, but there is comfort in the fact that these top project control inhibitors stem from implementing the project and are within the control of project management. They should therefore be easier to prevent or mitigate during project execution. These leading project control inhibitors would have been more difficult to manage had they been external to the project, for example, political or social factors. Interestingly, the lowly ranked inhibitors to effective cost and time control are mainly exogenous factors buttressing the fact that the internal environment and organization surrounding the delivery of a project are very important when it comes to controlling projects effectively for success.

Good Practice Checklist to Mitigate the Most Common Project Control Inhibitors

Following the identification of the leading project control inhibitors, several mitigating good practices have been established to address potential problems caused by the top five project control inhibitors. A classification system was developed for good practice mitigating measures according to the broad function they perform and is discussed below.

Preventive Good Practice Measures

These are precautionary good practice measures that are put in place as a defence against the project control inhibitors. Most of these good practice measures are active measures that would be instituted during the planning stage of a project. For example, a preventive good practice measure against the problem of design and scope changes relating to the cost and time of projects is to ensure that the project is designed in detail at the outset, while a preventive measure for risk and uncertainty is to identify properly the project risks before the project starts and devise a strategy for managing them should they materialize.

Predictive Good Practice Measures

These may seem like preventive good practice measures, but they are not the same. Predictive good practices are put in place in order to spot potential problems in the control process in the future so that they can be stopped from happening or they can be prepared for should they happen. Most of these good practice measures utilize some tools or techniques to investigate the current situation in a bid to spot potential future problems. For example, using 6D modeling (3D plus time, cost, and maintenance dimensions) to test how the plan will work out is a predictive measure that could be used for the mitigation of complexity of works and cost implications.

Corrective Good Practice Measures

These are good practice measures that are utilized to mitigate the effect of the project control inhibitors by acting as a remedy. These measures are reactive measures that are only implemented after the event. They may not be as proactive as preventive or predictive good practice measures, but they aim to bring the situation back on track or at least "stop the rot." These good practices have also been classified further as: (i) corrective-preventive measures, which are meant to correct departures and, in the process, prevent future problems, and (ii) corrective-predictive measures, which remedy the current situation but then go on to predict what the situation is going to be in the future using current information.

Organizational Good Practice Measures

These good practice measures generally encompass practices that go wider than the actual control process but influence project control; they are normally in place because of the company's belief, orientation, management style, or philosophy; they have a tendency of not being specific to one project but would normally affect all projects being undertaken by the company as they reflect how the wider organization works. A good example is the philosophy of the company in relation to partnering and collaborative working.

Fluidity, Flexibility, and Scalability of the Good Practice Mitigating Checklist

Some good practice measures are fluid and can sometimes look as though they can be classified into more than one category depending on their actual usage during the project. Consequently, this classification is not set in stone and just forms the basis of an organization trying to bring some structure to good practice measures developed for its project control effort. Similarly, the good practice measures can be expanded as required, and as discussed in Chapter 4, they can be used as a blueprint by organizations to develop additional good practice measures as appropriate to their projects and organizations. However, most of the good practice measures already suggested by the PCIM methodology for each of the leading five project control inhibitors will be applicable to most organizations and their projects.

Mitigating Good Practice Measures for Design and Scope Changes

Design and scope change is overwhelmingly the top project control inhibitor from the research that underpins the PCIM methodology, where it was unearthed as being a major obstacle to effective project cost and time control. The main issues that make design and scope changes a leading inhibitor to effective project control are as follows:

- The impact of a design and scope change on project cost and schedule is often underestimated.
- The design group is often not able to provide the project information in time, which results in the difficulty of design management.

- Project strategies have led to a general decline in the production of detailed design, which is perceived as one of the greatest causes of design and scope changes, especially with the increased usage of the design and build procurement route.
- Lack of detailed design and specification leads to the contractors delivering projects adding the cost of the risks that may occur from an immature design to the price of delivering the work but also looking for every loophole in the specification document to increase prices or reduce specifications, which affect cost and scope control.
- There is a lack of clear distinction between design change and design development (see chapter 9 for more on design change and design development). As a result, project partners often argue whether a design change is a change or a development where there would not be the need for additional cost and time compensation.

A host of good practices that can be employed by practitioners to mitigate the effect of design and scope changes on project cost and time control are presented in Table 5.3. Some of these include simple practices like ensuring that the time and cost implication of any design or scope change is evaluated fully before sanctioning or agreeing to the change. There should always be an efficient analysis of the consequential or "domino" effect of a design or scope change as one change can lead to others. Having a design manager who manages the design change process will also enable the preceding mitigating practices to be implemented easily. There should always be a clear and agreed differentiation between a design change and a design development as this is often a woolly issue that hampers the project control process. It will also be beneficial for the project control process if design or scope changes are requested or made only by authorized persons.

Mitigating Good Practice Measures for Risks and Uncertainties

Risks denote future uncertain factors that may have an adverse effect on the achievement of the project objectives. Project risk management as

Table 5.3 Mitigating good practice measures for design and scope changes

	Practice	Type of mitigating good practice
1	Clear distinction between a design change and a design development at the outset of a project	Preventive
2	Ensuring the cause of a design or scope change is always determined	Corrective-predictive
3	Determination and understanding by all relevant project parties of the provision of the design or scope change within the standard form of contract or bespoke contract used on the project	Corrective
4	Identification of potential design and scope changes as a key risk and devising a strategy for managing this risk, especially in design and build/execute projects	Predictive
5	Ensuring the time and cost implication of a design and scope change is always determined, validated/peer-reviewed, and agreed before going ahead with the change whenever possible	Corrective-preventive
6	Notification of all the relevant project parties of how they will be impacted and the schedule and cost implication of a design or scope change before going ahead with the change	Preventive
7	Freezing the design at the appropriate stage of the project or implementing intermediate design freezes at various project stages depending on the type of contract in use for the project	Preventive
8	Designing the project to a good level of detail at the outset whenever possible	Preventive
9	Provision/allocation of enough resources (manhours, labor, equipment, etc.) to cope with a design or scope change	Corrective
10	Design and scope changes should be adequately highlighted and updated on all relevant project documentation (e.g., drawings, specifications, schedules, reports, etc.)	Preventive
11	Agreeing and putting in place change management procedure that is clear and communicated to all project parties before the commencement of projects (incorporating this into the contract if possible)	Organizational
12	Ensuring prompt resolution to design and scope change queries, issues, and authorization requests	Preventive
13	Capturing all design or scope change on a register or change management IT system with corresponding cost and schedule implication for discussion during project team meetings	Corrective-predictive

Table 5.3 Continued

	Practice	Type of mitigating good practice
14	Having a standardized change request template (manual or systemized), with standard information input such as justification of the change, source of change, estimate backup, review, approval process, etc.	Organizational
15	Having a design manager where possible with responsibility for the management of the design and scope change process and reviewing related information as they come in	Preventive
16	Ensuring no one makes a design or scope change without the knowledge and authorization of the relevant project party, for example, client representative or project manager as appropriate	Preventive
17	Open discussion by the relevant project party before the project starts about how design and scope changes will be managed and incorporating this into the contract if possible	Organizational
18	Efficient analysis of the direct and indirect consequence (domino effect) of a design or scope change on other activities or areas of the project as one change can precipitate other changes	Corrective-predictive
19	Ensuring design changes are reasonably timed when possible, for example, late design changes may greatly impact the ability to control the project cost and schedule	Preventive

a topic is addressed in this section and covered in detail in Chapter 11. What this section does is to bring to light the key themes on how risks and uncertainties inhibit the ability of practitioners to control the cost and time of their projects effectively and the good practices that can be used to mitigate this problem. The key themes from the research that informed the PCIM project control methodology are as follows:

- Early identification of risk at the outset of a project is essential for project cost, scope, and time control to be effective.
- Risks and uncertainties are not often managed using sophisticated quantitative risk management systems; rather, risks are identified through brainstorming sessions, risk workshops, and analyzed qualitatively.

- The risk register is the most used tool for risk management, but most times, this is not kept a live document through regular review. Quite frequently, it is left as an idle document and this does not bode well for effective project control.
- Risks are quite often not allocated a cost and time implication during risk management and this can often make it difficult to assess their impact on the cost and time objectives of projects during control.

The common good practices that were established as part of the PCIM methodology for the mitigation of the problem of risk and uncertainties during project control are shown in Table 5.4. For example, it is

Table 5.4 Mitigating measures for risks and uncertainties

	Practice	Type of mitigating good practice
20	Having a risk register or a risk management IT system in place for the project as early as possible (e.g., from tender stage)	Preventive
21	Having a documented risk management procedure with details on the procedures for risk classification, identifying risks, analyzing risk, risk mitigation requirement, risk monitoring, and risk reporting to enable proper and consistent identification, allocation, and management of risks	Preventive
22	Assigning cost and/or time implication to all identified risks on the risk register whenever possible	Predictive
23	Using all the risks (costed) for the project to develop the cost contingency allowance for the project cost budget and not an arbitrary percentage contingency allowance	Preventive
24	Ensuring the risk register is open to all relevant members of the project team	Preventive
25	Having a strategy already developed for solving each of the identified risks in case they come to fruition	Corrective
26	Conducting a risk workshop involving all relevant project parties at the outset of the project to identify potential risks	Predictive
27	Encouraging, emphasizing, and striving for a risk-sharing regime when possible It may aid in buttressing partnership and openness among the project parties	Organizational

Table 5.4 Continued

	Practice	Type of mitigating good practice
28	Risks not being used to mask project problems or deficiency in planning the project properly	Organizational
29	Ensuring risk management is a sincere and open exercise	Organizational
30	Looking out for opportunities to improve cost and time performance during risk analysis	Corrective
31	The risk register not being solely kept in the corporate office but communicated to the project management and any site delivery team as well	Organizational
32	Reviewing the risk register at all relevant progress meetings including meetings with the site/project-based team	Organizational
33	Installing a governance process within the organization so that the identified project risks are reported, validated, and monitored periodically at a higher management level within the organization	Organizational
34	Making sure the risk register contains live information that is updated regularly	Predictive
35	Running a risk analysis on the schedule and cost using a quantitative schedule risk analysis (QSRA) and quantitative cost risk analysis (QCRA) respectively on the projects at an early stage and periodically when possible	Predictive
36	Risks that are closed out on the risk register not taken off but used to inform as the progress ensues, and on other projects	Predictive

important to move away from just identification of risk without knowing their cost and time implication; the identified risk should be allocated a cost and time implication when possible.

Mitigating Good Practice Measures for Inaccurate Evaluation of Project Time Duration

The whole essence of controlling a project is to ensure delivery within a predetermined time and evaluating how long it will take to complete a project is the starting point of project control because it serves as a baseline to measure against. The research that informed the PCIM project control methodology showed the following key themes in relation to this project control inhibitor:

- The main reason why inaccurate evaluation of project time/ duration emerged as one of the leading inhibitors to effective project cost and time control is that project time is often evaluated without any scientific basis; quite often schedules are drawn up on gut feeling.
- Project contractors are usually under pressure from clients to deliver projects, especially commercial speculative projects, within unachievable timescales, which are often accepted by the professional team without a clear idea of how they will be achieved, leading to project overruns and ultimately client dissatisfaction.
- Schedules are often developed by inexperienced project planners or by those that have only become project planners because of their expertise in the use of scheduling software packages. However, they do not have a good appreciation of the technical process of the projects, for example, software development process, process engineering, and construction process, and this leaves much to be desired in the schedules produced.

Table 5.5 shows the good practices for mitigation of this leading project control inhibitor. The most important mitigating good practice measure is obviously ensuring that the project time forecast and cost budget are realistic in the first place because if they are not, then controlling the project's time is already a lost cause. Client advisers, consultants, and contractors should have the courage to refuse unrealistic timescale by clients, enlightening them if a timescale is not achievable. It is also important that project planners are well trained and have a good appreciation of the execution processes of the type of projects they are working on, for example, software development, construction process, and process engineering as appropriate. The time forecast (schedule) should also not be developed on "gut feeling." It should be based on quantifiable metrics based on resource requirements and augmented by experience.

Table 5.5 **Mitigating measures for inaccurate evaluation of project time duration**

	Practice	Type of mitigating good
37	Having a documented schedule development methodology and process with information on how to develop the schedule and develop technical aspects such as critical path, work breakdown structure, and so on	Organizational
38	Ensuring the project planner is well trained in the key processes involved in delivering the project they are scheduling	Organizational
39	Preparation of the project schedule with input from the project delivery/production team	Preventive
40	Having regular schedule integration meetings during the project to enable the schedules of suppliers and subcontractors at all levels and their critical activities to be coordinated and integrated to avoid schedule conflicts	Preventive
41	Developing the project schedule using science-based methods augmented by experience and not relying on gut feeling alone	Preventive
42	Educating and advising the client on alternatives if an unachievable/unrealistic project timescale is stipulated	Preventive
43	Having the courage to refuse unrealistic project timescales by clients who are unwilling to yield to professional advise	Organizational
44	Developing the project schedule using experienced planners who have an appreciation of the various project disciplines/areas of the projects they are working on	Preventive
45	Having a process for validating/peer reviewing and approving developed schedules	Preventive
46	Conducting a process mapping, visualization and benchmarking exercise to validate the time allocated to a project	Predictive
47	Ensuring enough time is allocated during tender planning for the proper development of the project schedule	Preventive
48	Making sure when possible that the project schedule is developed by or in conjunction with someone who is experienced in the relevant type of project	Preventive
49	Swiftly informing the relevant project parties if unforeseen circumstances affect the schedule/lead-in times	Corrective
50	Making sure the schedule is built up from the first principles using metrics of how long typical activities take rather than using assessment only (ensuring that the time allocated to activities is quantifiable)	Preventive

(Continued)

Table 5.5 (Continued)

	Practice	Type of mitigating good
51	Avoiding optimism bias and strategic misrepresentation in the development of the schedule so that the timescale produced for projects is a true reflection of the actual time required for the project's scope and not an underestimation to secure funding and authorization to proceed	Preventive
52	Having a process in place to formally review and approve schedule changes and assessing the impact of schedule changes	Corrective-predictive

Mitigating Good Practice Measures for Complexity of Works

Project complexity is the inherent characteristic of a project such as the technical requirements, components interfaces, organizational structure, political context, financial structure, environmental challenges, novelty, and so on. It makes the project difficult to manage and deliver. Most projects, for example, high-speed rail infrastructure, health IT, nuclear energy facility, or organization technology transformation projects, to mention but a few, usually involve some form of complexity. This inherent complexity can sometimes present a challenge for effective cost, scope, and time control of these complex projects. Research by Luo, He, Xie, Yang, and Wu (2017) has shown that project complexity has a negative effect on project success. It is therefore no surprise to see complexity of works ranked as one of the top inhibitors to effective project control from the PCIM project control methodology research. The prevalent issues that emanated from the PCIM project control methodology research include the following:

- Interface issues in projects, for example, the interface of different project stages, phases, or different work packages/aspects of the project are often the main cause of complexity during the implementation of projects.
- Complex projects are often not understood adequately before embarking on them and this only increases the negative effect of complexity during project cost and time control.

- Not understanding how the complexities involved in a project are interrelated, which is vital for the management of the whole project delivery/execution process, is another reason why complexity is so detrimental to effective project control.
- Adequate planning is essential for mitigating the effect of complexity of project works, but enough time is often not made available for planning due to the haste of commencing the execution of the project.

Table 5.6 shows the full list of the mitigating good practice measures developed as part of the PCIM methodology for the complexity of works. Mitigation of complexity of works can be done in various ways, but at the heart of any mitigating practice is adequate planning. To control complex projects effectively, it will do no harm if the project is understood properly by having a detailed review of all information relating to the project. A project execution plan (PEP) should be developed, and the project should also be broken down into manageable chunks if possible. In-house and/ or external expertise in the area of complexity should also be procured for the planning, monitoring, and control of complex projects instead of using staff with generic experience on such projects.

Nonperformance of Subcontractors

The importance of subcontractors and suppliers cannot be overemphasized in projects. For example, IT projects involve procuring software packages from software development vendors or development of bespoke software packages using specialist software development companies and sometimes working with an "army" of software contractors and consultants in implementing the IT projects. Examples of such projects include the failed UK National Health Service (NHS) IT system upgrade 2002–2013 and the UK COVID-19 test and trace system in 2020, to mention but two. This is similar for other types of projects, for example, in construction projects where main contractors divide the majority of the project into work packages for subcontractors to deliver and the main

Table 5.6 Mitigating good practice measures for the complexity of works

	Practice	Type of mitigating good practice
53	Breaking the project down into manageable chunks	Preventive
54	Making sure the project is understood properly before embarking on it	Preventive
55	Detailed review of the information relating to the work before embarking on it	Preventive
56	Development a project execution plan for the project before starting on it	Preventive
57	Having enough resources to deal with the complexity	Corrective
58	Allocating to the project experienced personnel who have handled similar types of complexity in the past	Preventive
59	Incorporating longer lead-in time/sufficient time for complex works or phases of the project	Preventive
60	Ensuring as much design as possible is done for the complex work or project before commencing	Preventive
61	Ensuring adequate coordination of design and activities preceding and following the complex work—use collaborative IT tools to improve communication and coordination	Preventive
62	Calling in specialists to advise and contribute to the planning and management of complex works/projects	Preventive
63	Utilizing in-house expertise for the management of complex projects	Preventive
64	Conducting workshops and brainstorming session to generate ideas and for problems solving before and during the complex work/project	Predictive
65	Utilizing regular "what if" analysis and scenario planning to understand better the various aspects of the complexity	Preventive
66	Overlaying a risk analysis process specifically for a complex phase or activity in a project	Predictive
67	Ensuring where possible and practical that one team runs with the complex work/project from beginning to the end	Organizational
68	Thinking holistically when planning a complex project by considering logistics and interfaces, for example, having a predelivery services department that will not only plan the project but take a holistic look at the project rather than just having planning department as customary	Preventive
69	Ensuring that when subcontractors are needed, the subcontractor with the capability to deal with the complexity is procured for the project	Preventive

(Continued)

Table 5.6 Continued

	Practice	Type of mitigating good practice
70	Constantly monitoring the progress and being open-minded to improving the schedule and cost plan as things become clearer and to other options available	Predictive
71	Benchmarking using similar projects and getting as much information on the complex part of the project and sequence all activities	Predictive
72	Ensuring every element of the design has an aspect on the program and using a 5-D modeling (3-D plus time and cost dimension) to show how the work will be built (i.e., have a plan and test it to see how it works and what it will cost)	Predictive
73	Ensuring that when a complex project is broken down into manageable chunks how the complexities interact with each other is understood	Preventive
74	Building in the risk of delay and higher cost allowances for complex projects	Preventive

contractor carries out the overall integration and project management of works. Other focal issues that emanated from the PCIM project control methodology development research in relation to nonperformance of subcontractors are detailed below:

- Nonperformance of subcontractors was found to be a major obstacle to effective project control, but attention must be drawn to the fact that, quite often, this is not necessarily the fault of the subcontractors and suppliers but may be due to a lack of effective management by the main contractor. For example, not properly communicating the objective of the project to a subcontractor or not being able to identify nonperformance early enough.
- The importance of a good working relationship between the contractor and subcontractors/suppliers is considered essential in project control; the intensity of this relationship varies considerably in practice ranging from the most formal kind such as partnering contracts or framework agreements,

to very loose forms such as just allowing subcontractors to use the same welfare facilities as the main contractor's staff.

- Supply chain management is a widespread practice with many project contractors having an ongoing relationship with subcontractors and suppliers in the hope of getting a slightly better level of service than normal including better performance.
- Project contractors are vigilant about the financial buoyancy of potential subcontractors to ensure they are financially secure and will not go bankrupt or underperform because of lack of capital quoting the COVID-19 pandemic and consequential economic impact, construction material inflation, and supply chain disruption in 2020 and 2021.
- The contractual route of determining/terminating the appointment of a subcontractor is only taken as a last resort when a subcontractor is underperforming; other measures are often initially explored in a bid to remedy the situation.

The full list of the PCIM methodology measures for the mitigation of the problem of nonperformance of subcontractors during project control is presented in Table 5.7. Having a committed supply chain selected through a stringent selection process will do the project control process a whole lot of good, especially as it relates to minimizing the likelihood of nonperformance of subcontractors, which is a leading project control inhibitor. There should also be a good monitoring regime in place that can identify nonperformance by subcontractors early on to nip it in the bud as quickly as possible. Subcontractors should also be properly directed to know what to do and what is expected of them. Furthermore, early engagement of subcontractors will do no harm to the control process as it provides for timescales to be developed in consultation with them and potential problems can be identified and eliminated. It could also be beneficial to integrate the subcontractors properly with the contractor's team as this can foster trust and partnership, enhance communication, and improve the quality of information used for project control.

Table 5.7 *Mitigating good practice measures for nonperformance of subcontractors*

	Practice	Type of mitigating good practice
75	Properly directing the subcontractors and suppliers to ensure they know what is expected of them in relation to the project	Preventive
76	Developing a good working relationship with subcontractors and suppliers	Organizational
77	Putting a process in place for early identification of nonperformance in subcontract works/packages to nip it in the bud as soon as possible	Predictive
78	Having a supplier management IT system with the ability to provide real-time information and reporting on suppliers	Predictive
79	Utilizing performance measurements, for example, S-curve, key performance indicators (KPI) to monitor the output/performance of subcontractors on their work package	Predictive
80	Ensuring there is a committed supply chain that can be used	Organizational
81	Having a process in place that mutually allows nonperforming subcontractors to be removed from the supply chain	Corrective
82	Ensuring there is a partnering/collaborative relationship with the subcontractor (this may ensure the subcontractor gives a better than normal service)	Organizational
83	Integration of subcontractors into the site management team (where possible, practicable and feasible) all through the course of the work	Organizational
84	Incorporating a progress-performance-payment rule in the subcontract where possible, for example, that stipulates a certain amount can only be earned/paid when certain requirements have been met/a stage has been achieved in the project	Preventive
85	Having a stringent process in place for selecting subcontractors into the supply chain	Organizational
86	Involving where possible, subcontractors doing major/critical part of the project with the internal planning process, that is, early involvement of relevant subcontractors, for example, at pretender stage in order to advise on design before having cost and time implications (early engagement)	Preventive
87	Ensure there is a prompt system of payment to subcontractors for the job that has been done (this boosts morale and may prevent any financial difficulty for the subcontractor)	Organizational

(*Continued*)

Table 5.7 Continued

	Practice	Type of mitigating good practice
88	Build relationship and communication at the management/ board level of the subcontractors' companies	Organizational
89	Holding good value of retention on serial nonperforming subcontractors and suppliers as it may serve as a deterrent/ used to remedy any nonperformance issue that may occur	Corrective
90	Reduction of the retention for trusted and the best-performing subcontractors	Organizational
91	Finding and understanding the root cause of any nonperformance and working with the subcontractor to see how to be of help	Corrective
92	Going through the different layers of the subcontractor's management to ensure that a nonperformance situation is improved	Corrective
93	Avoiding the selection of the cheapest subcontractors if there is doubt on their performance track record	Preventive
94	Taking time to understand the implementation strategy a subcontractor intends to adopt for a subcontract package and ensuring it fits well with the cost, scope, and time performance requirements of the project	Predictive
95	Making sure subcontractors are allocated adequate time to complete subcontract work packages	Preventive
96	Seeing the benefits in having a small but quality, closely knit supply chain that is well known rather than having a large supply chain where subcontractors are hardly known	Organizational
97	Sharing with individual subcontractors and suppliers their KPI results and reviewing their weaknesses with them so that they can improve on them going forward	Corrective-preventive
98	Having a knowledge of the best projects the company's subcontractors are best able to undertake and allocate this to them and avoid giving a subcontractor projects they are not good at	Preventive
99	Having a training system/regime in place for subcontractors in order to indoctrinate them in the ways of the company, for example, control processes, tools, and techniques (and they will have no excuses to say they don't know what you want)	Organizational
100	Having more than one subcontractor for a particular type of work/trade/package to encourage healthy competition	Organizational

Conclusion

The research that informed the development of the PCIM project control methodology found that the five leading project cost control inhibitors are also the five leading project time control inhibitors, albeit in slightly different order. These project control inhibitors are (1) design and scope changes; (2) risks and uncertainties; (3) inaccurate evaluation of project time/duration; (4) complexity of works; and (5) nonperformance of subcontractors. Design and scope change is the single most important factor hindering the ability to control not only the time of construction projects but also their cost.

Following the identification of the project control inhibitors, several mitigating good practice measures have been established by the PCIM project control methodology to address potential problems caused by the top five project control inhibitors. For example, it was highlighted that there has been a general decline in the production of a detailed design for projects. This is perceived as one of the greatest causes of design and scope changes, the foremost bottleneck during the project control process. Quite often, there is also a lack of distinction between a design change and a design development, leading to arguments among project partners. This led to the development of several mitigating good practices for design and scope changes to enable effective project control, for example, "designing the project in great detail at the outset whenever possible," "clear distinction between a design change and a design development at the outset of a project," and so on.

Clients and project owners can also contribute to inhibiting effective project control by imposing unachievable and unrealistic timescales in relation to the delivery of their projects. Therefore, several good practice measures were developed to mitigate this, some of these include "educating and advising client on alternative if an unachievable/unrealistic project timescale is stipulated," "having the courage to refuse unrealistic project timescale by clients unwilling to yield to professional advice."

It was also asserted that, quite often, the nonperformance of subcontractors is not necessarily the fault of subcontractors but due to lack of effective management by the main contractor. The mitigating good practice measures that stemmed from this issue include "properly directing the subcontractor to ensure they know what is expected of them in relation to the project," "putting a system in place for early identification of nonperformance in subcontract works/packages in order to curtail the nonperformance as soon as possible," and "utilizing performance measurements for example S-curve (see Chapter 8) and KPI to monitor the output/performance of subcontractors on their work package."

In conclusion, the project control inhibitors mitigating good practice measures established from the research that underpins the development of the PCIM project control methodology were broadly classified as preventive, predictive, corrective, and organizational measures. These mitigating good practice measures are scalable and are by no means exhaustive. Therefore, as discussed in Chapter 4, organizations can use the PCIM methodology as a blueprint and adapt it to their projects including adding relevant project control inhibitors mitigating good practices that may not have made the list presented in this chapter but considered relevant to an organization's project control practice.

CHAPTER 6

Good Practices for the Cyclic Project Control Steps

Planning, Monitoring, Reporting, and Analyzing

Introduction

The second set of good practices included within the PCIM project control methodology relates to the project control cycle (planning, monitoring, reporting, and analyzing). Project control is not a one-time event; it usually involves several distinctive steps as explained in previous chapters (see Chapters 1–3) and summarized below.

- *Planning*: This is the task to determine project objectives and activities needed to achieve these objectives. Time schedules are decided by sequencing the project activities, with interim milestones. At the same time, detailed cost estimates and cost plans are also produced. A WBS (see Chapter 9 for more on WBS) is also produced to plan the scope of work that is to be delivered. In addition to the time plan (schedule), cost plan, and scope plan, other types of plans are developed for a project such as the PEP, quality plan, communication plan, and stakeholder management plan, and so on (see Chapter 2 for more on planning).

- *Monitoring*: Once the execution of project plans starts, progress of the project needs to be monitored to verify that activities are carried out as planned and costs and spending occur for the correct amount, at the correct time, and for the right scope of work. Any variations to cost, scope, and time plans need to be identified.

- *Reporting*: The information gathered during the monitoring step will need to be presented in some agreed format and transmitted via the appropriate medium to the appropriate department or personnel for further action, for example, analysis. The report contains the information collected during monitoring and an analysis of this information shows the status of the project as described below.
- *Analyzing*: Having gathered the data, the team must determine whether the project is behaving as predicted, and if not, calculate the size and impact of the variances.

It is important to note that this is a simplistic view of the project control steps as project control is a complex process that requires human interventions, decisions, and practices as explained in Chapters 2 to 5. The PCIM project control methodology asserts that it is not enough to develop a framework for project control without supporting it with a comprehensive set of good practices. To this effect, the PCIM project control methodology is accompanied by several good practices including many that are deemed important to the major steps of the project control cycle (see Tables 6.1–6.4). Additionally, this set of good practice checklists also contains the relevant tools and techniques recommended for the practices where relevant. It is important to point out that despite the fact that the PCIM project control methodology emerged from a construction/infrastructure project sector, the good practices discussed in this chapter will be applicable to other industries, especially as they focus on the project control cycle steps which are universal and therefore generic to all industries.

The Delphi Process: Validating the Good Practices

The significance (critical, important, helpful, or unhelpful) of each of the good practices to the project control steps is also provided in this chapter. The significance of each of the good practices was determined using the Delphi technique during the research that informed the development of the PCIM project control methodology. The Delphi technique was named after the ancient Greek oracle of Delphi where omens of the future could be enquired (Flostrand, Pitt, and Bridson 2020). The modern-day Delphi is a statistical technique used to gain reliable consensus on a particular topic using rounds of questionnaires provided to experts in the field with controlled feedback to the experts after each round of questionnaire until a consensus is reached (Chalmers and Armour 2019). The questionnaires are completed anonymously by the experts and as part of the process; their responses for a round are analyzed and the result presented back to each expert to reconsider their opinion in the next round based on the group result of the previous round. This process continues until a consensus is reached.

The original Delphi method, according to Flostrand et al. (2020), was developed in 1948 by Norman Dalkey at the RAND Corporation, as part of a U.S. military intelligence project due to the cold war tensions which created a need for the U.S. military to predict the nuclear weaponry capacity and targeting strategies of the Soviet Union. Although it was originally used on military projects, Sourani and Sohail (2015) pointed out that the application of Delphi is now widespread and has been used in many areas including health care and medical research, academia, social policy, administration, agriculture, automotive, banking, criminal justice, economics, education, environmental studies, business and finance, housing, insurance, strategic planning, tourism, transportation, and utilities. The key characteristics required for a Delphi process have been stated by Shariff (2015) as use of an expert panel, iteration of rounds and controlled feedback, statistical summaries of group response, anonymity, and consensus building.

The success of a Delphi study is dependent on the collective expertise of the participants. Therefore, it was important that the PCIM research methodology utilized the appropriate people for the Delphi process. A purposeful process was used for the selection of experts for the PCIM research Delphi panel using the criteria below:

- Experts must have participated in the earlier interviewing process (see chapter one for an overview of the overall PCIM research process) so that they already understand what the research is about.

- Experts must have more than 10 years of experience in project planning, project control, and project management of construction projects.
- Experts must be committed to participate in all the Delphi rounds.

A total of eight construction project practitioners from the 15 that participated in the interviews from the previous stage of the research agreed to participate in the Delphi process. The Delphi does not call for experts to be representative samples for statistical purposes. The quality and experience of the expert panel are more important than the quantity. Therefore, the eight experts participating in this study were deemed appropriate.

The experts held positions that are relevant to project control within their respective organizations. All the experts held senior positions in the planning, project control, or project management departments of their organizations. The expert panel was made up of very experienced practitioners, with six of the eight experts having more than 25 years of experience. The total experience of the eight experts was 227 years (average experience of 28 years).

The good practices developed as part of the PCIM project control methodology for each of the steps of the project control cycle, any accompanying tools and techniques, and their determined level of importance are presented in Tables 6.1 to 6.4 and discussed in the following sections.

Project Control Cycle "Planning Step" Good Practices

Planning as a project control step is critical to the project control process; this is because planning is required to implement the other project control steps. Effective project control system relies on two fundamental components: (1) a plan against which progress can be measured (and any deviation assessed) and (2) timely and accurate information about what is happening (or likely to happen) on the project. The PCIM project control methodology includes many good practices to support the planning step of the cyclical project control process as detailed in Table 6.1. Many of the good practices that were put forward to support the planning step were also determined as critical to the project control process.

Table 6.1 Project control cycle planning step good practice checklist

	Practice	Significance	Relevant tools and/or techniques
1	Development of a good schedule/program of works for the project time estimate	Critical	• Scheduling techniques, (e.g., Gantt chart, network diagrams (see Chapter 7 for more on this)) • Utilizing planning/project management software (e.g., Primevera P6, MS Projects, Asta Power Project)
2	Setting of tangible milestones within the developed project schedule	Critical	• Milestone programming technique (see Chapter 7 for more on this)
3	Establishing a clearly identifiable critical path on the program	Critical	• Critical path method (see Chapter 7 for more on this)
4	Involvement of the key subcontractors early for advice and input when developing the program	Critical	
5	Utilization of a project planner who has an appreciation of the delivery process of the type of project they are working on	Critical	
6	Embracing a holistic approach during the development of the project schedule	Critical	
7	Making sure the project schedule is realistic for example by benchmarking to previous similar projects	Critical	
8	Knowledge of the impact/relationship of not finishing on time and increased project cost	Critical	• Earned value analysis (see Chapter 8 for more on this)
9	Proper handover of the tender from the tender quantity surveyor (QS) or cost professional to the Project QS or cost professional to ensure understanding of how the project is priced	Critical	

(Continued)

Table 6.1 *(Continued)*

	Practice	Significance	Relevant tools and/or techniques
10	Making sure the cost budget is always realistic for example by benchmarking to previous similar projects in similar countries	Critical	
11	Development of the project schedule to a good level of detail	Important	• Work breakdown structure (see Chapter 9 for more on this) • Primavera P6
12	Having a separate target schedule that is more ambitious than the contractual master schedule	Important	
13	Building in some flexibility into the project schedule if possible	Important	
14	Utilization of historical data when developing a project schedule	Important	
15	Ascertaining that there is a procurement strategy for buying all packages in the project at the tender stage	Important	• Bill of quantities, cost plan • Excel spreadsheet, bespoke software packages, MS project, Asta Power Project
16	Making sure all activities/packages in the project have their allocated cost for carrying out the works	Important	• Cost plan • Cost breakdown structure
17	Making sure the project team understands the cost budget	Important	
18	Development of the cost estimate/budget using quantifiable metrics (e.g., cost/m² of brick laid etc.)	Important	• Historic data, current published cost data
19	Having an agreed price with the client that will be used for variations	Important	
20	Making sure the project team members are trained in the science of project cost and time control	Important	

21	Integrating cost and time control all the time	Important	• Earned value technique (see Chapter 8 for more on this) • Power project, MS project, Primavera P6
22	Making sure there is enough time from tender acceptance to starting on site to properly plan the work	Important	
23	Making sure the project schedule and cost estimate are updated as the design evolves until the design sign-off	Important	
24	Establishment of a structure within the project control process aligning the cost breakdown structure with the work breakdown structure	Important	• Earned value technique (see Chapter 8 for more on this) • Scheduling software
25	Making sure the project cost and time control process is consistent across the company	Important	• Project control quality system
26	Development of the project schedule using quantifiable metrics (e.g., bricks laid/m²/day)	Helpful	• Historic data, activity sampling and benchmarking
27	Testing the viability of the project schedule using 4-D (3-D with time dimension) virtual reality model	Helpful	• Modeling software package • Schedule
28	Utilization of an agreed maximum price contract when possible	Helpful	

From Table 6.1, it is also evident that effective planning during the project control process also relies on several tools and techniques as put forward by the PCIM project control methodology. Many of these techniques such as CPM and Gantt chart are discussed in Chapter 7. Some of the good practices identified for planning as part of the PCIM project control methodology are the development of a good schedule for the project using some of the scheduling techniques such as the common Gantt bar chart developed with planning software package such as Primevera P6. However, in parallel with the underlying philosophy of the PCIM project control methodology, it is recognized that just developing a project schedule is not enough for the success of this step of the project control process. As such, any developed schedule needs to incorporate good planning practices as suggested by the PCIM project control methodology such as involvement of key subcontractors in the development of the schedule if possible, and establishment of a clear and identifiable critical path on the schedule using the CPM. In relation to the cost element of the project control planning step, practices such as development of the cost estimate using quantifiable metrics, making sure the project delivery team understands the cost budget so that the work is properly managed later, and having an agreed price set in the contract that will be utilized for pricing variations are some of the practices put forward by PCIM project control methodology.

Project Control "Monitoring Step" Good Practices

Monitoring is the means of keeping track of all project performance metrics including spending, duration of activities, resource utilization, performance of subcontractors, progress toward important milestones, and so on. Monitoring facilitates the project management team to oversee all activities associated with the successful delivery of the project to understand whether the project is progressing as planned. However, the monitoring step during project control, as discussed previously in Chapter 3, can sometimes be overlooked, unsystematic, and informal. Yet, with dedicated effort and embracing some good practices, monitoring can be implemented effectively during the project control process.

The PCIM project control methodology for project control identified many critical and important good practices to support the project control monitoring step. Some of these include ascertaining that there is a formal and periodic monitoring regime embedded in the project. This will formalize the monitoring step and bring some structure into the monitoring step of the project control process. Good practices were also put forward in relation to what to monitor to enable effective project (cost, scope, and time) control. For example, monitoring time progress against the project's critical path and monitoring design and scope changes (especially as design and scope change has been identified as the leading inhibitor for cost and time control by the PCIM research). The benefit of monitoring design and scope changes on a project is that it will highlight if the project is veering toward scope creep, which can lead to time overrun and cost escalation.

Monitoring short-term and medium-term cash flow is also considered important. The incorporation of some independence in the monitoring process (such as an independent review) is also advocated as a good practice for the monitoring step of project control. Having an independent review does not mean that the monitoring responsibility should be removed from the project delivery team, but the PCIM project control methodology suggests that an additional independent monitoring by someone outside the delivery team happens periodically to provide some objectivity, checks, and peer review of the project delivery team's view of the performance of the project.

Project Control "Reporting Step" Good Practices

Reporting during the project control process is used to provide information about the project to the members of the project team and the project stakeholders as appropriate. The information shared during the reporting stage is mainly in relation to the progress (time), scope, and cost of the project, although other project metrics like risks, opportunities, issues, resources usage, key milestones, dependencies, procurement, forecasts, and so on are also shared. In project control, reporting usually presents a comparison of the current key performance metrics of the project against the goals set out in the project's overall plan. Reporting also allows the

Table 6.2 Project control monitoring step good practices checklist

	Practice	Significance	Relevant tools and/or techniques
29	Making sure there is a regular monitoring regime (e.g., weekly/monthly) embedded in the project	Critical	• Progress reporting templates and weekly progress meetings
30	Monitoring the project time progress against the critical path at all times	Critical	• Critical path method (see Chapter 7 for more on this)
31	Constantly monitoring design changes to avoid escalation	Critical	• Gantt chart, milestone programming (see Chapter 7 for more on this)
32	Constantly monitoring against key milestones	Critical	• Gantt chart, milestone programming
33	Putting in place an independent regular monitoring of the project by someone apart from the project delivery team	Important	
34	Making sure there is a system for monitoring the efficiency of human resources, manhours/labor as part of the cost, scope, and time control process	Important	• KPIs, S-curves (see Chapter 8 for more on this)
35	Constantly monitoring short-term and medium-term cash flows	Important	
36	Specifying clearly what the deliverables of the project cost, scope, and time control will be to aid monitoring	Important	• Project control plan (PCP) (see Chapter 5 for more on this)
37	Daily/frequent monitoring of cost, scope, and time to identify potential risk areas early on	Important	• Progress reports
38	Making sure the people monitoring from the office regularly visit the project site	Important	
39	Proper knowledge of and agreeing the time and cost implication of any scope changes/variation to the project whenever possible before going ahead	Important	• Cost estimates, historic data, current published rates

40	Developing a project control manual that the site monitoring team can refer to in relation to the project control process	Important	• PCP
41	Making sure the project delivery personnel are trained in the project control monitoring process	Important	
42	Having a system in place that checks submitted subcontractors cost against actual work done/payment due	Important	• Cost–value comparison (see Chapter 7 for more on this), bespoke software, Excel spreadsheet
43	Monitoring that works are procured within the allocated allowance in the tender	Important	• Cost plan
44	Establishing regular project cost and time control progress meetings involving planners, QS, and the site project delivery team	Important	
45	Monitoring the project critical path using the S-curve	Helpful	• CPM, S-curves, Gantt chart (see Chapters 7 and 8 for more on these) • Scheduling software
46	Utilizing cash flow as a key monitoring tool during the project control process	Helpful	

Table 6.3 *Project control reporting step good practices checklist*

	Practice	Significance	Relevant tools and/or techniques
47	Making sure that the cost, scope, and time status information being reported is up-to-date and accessible by management	Critical	
48	Regular reporting of the project cost, scope, and time status	Critical	• Progress report templates • Reporting dashboards and IT-enabled reports
49	Accurately recording information	Critical	
50	Making sure the reporting is always honest and true	Critical	
51	Ensuring there is an open and trusting relationship between the project delivery team and project management office team to ensure reporting from the delivery team is honest and accurate	Critical	
52	Presentation of the report using quantitative tools (e.g., graphs, curves, and histograms)	Important	• S-curves, earned value technique (see Chapter 8 for more on this) • Excel spreadsheets, bespoke reporting software
53	Avoiding the use of complex IT manipulations that are difficult to decipher for reporting	Important	
54	Incorporating qualitative explanation into reports in addition to quantitative graphs and curves, so that the reason behind results can be properly understood	Important	

current issues and problems facing a project to be presented to the project stakeholders as well as the management actions planned or already in progress to deal with them.

The PCIM project control methodology has recommended many good practices that can be used to improve the reporting step of the project control process. For example, making sure that cost, scope, and time status metrics of projects are up-to-date and can be accessed by the senior management as close to real-time as possible. This is because if information about cost, scope, and time project metrics are delayed, it may be too late to act when the information is known eventually, and it shows that remedial actions are required. Putting in place measures and a culture that facilitates honest reporting reflecting the true status of the project is one of the critical practices advocated by the PCIM methodology. This is because honest and accurate reporting will lead to factual reports that will highlight the true challenges or opportunities of a project that require mitigation or exploitation, respectively. Additionally, the use of standardized project reporting tools such as reporting templates to bring consistency to the reports produced is also put forward. Similarly, the PCIM project control methodology also advocates, if possible, the use of computer software tools that are simple and noncomplicated to systematize and enable the reporting process.

Project Control "Analyzing Step" Good Practices

Analysis involves the review and use of various techniques as appropriate to establish the current trajectory of the project to understand whether the project is behaving as planned and predicted. Calculating and analyzing the metrics that have been designed to measure the performance of the project allows the magnitude of any variance in relation to the performance metrics to be established. Data gathered from the monitoring step can then be assessed to analyze the trends in relation to the effects of current effort and decisions on the project. The analysis step is also where the future performance of the projects can be forecast based on the current trajectory of the project and the forecast input (such as resources) to the project delivery process. This forecast can also be compared to the baseline metrics to establish the difference and unearth any

Table 6.4 Project control analyzing step good practices checklist

	Practice	Significance	Relevant tools and/or techniques
55	Having independent personnel at next higher management level to assess the results of the analysis to ascertain if it is optimistic, factual, or pessimistic	Critical	
56	Utilization of cost–value comparison when analyzing during project cost and time control	Important	• Earned value management, cost–value comparison (see chapter eight for more on this)
57	Ensuring cost, scope, and time are integrated during analysis	Important	• Earned value technique • WBS, CBS (see chapter eight for more on these)
58	Forecasting the completion time and cost at completion as part of the analyzing activity during project controls	Important	• Earned value technique (see chapter eight for more on this)
59	Ensuring that people are inclined to releasing information on time, especially cost information, to aid analysis	Important	
60	Determination of the cost for the period, value, and earned value and the cumulative so far when analyzing project progress	Helpful	• Earned value management, cost–value comparison (see Chapter 8 for more on this)
61	Analyzing performance using S-curves	Helpful	• S-curve (see Chapter 8 for more on this)

62	Conducting trend analysis to identify trends early on	Helpful	• Computer simulation • Excel spreadsheet
63	Focusing on the efficiency of human resources, manhours/labor when analyzing project cost and time control	Helpful	• Earned value technique
64	Modeling cost and time when analyzing using a 5-D model to visualize (how the design develops (3-D), how time is being expended (4-D), and how the cost develops (5-D)	Helpful	• Modeling software package
65	Having an individual or single department responsible for both cost and time control (e.g., a project control manager rather than having a separate scheduling/ time management department and a separate cost/quantity surveying department each controlling time and cost separately)	Helpful	

potential problems awaiting the project in order to take remedial actions if required.

The PCIM project control methodology recommends many important practices to support the analysis step of the project control process. One of the most important practices advocated is ensuring that cost and time are integrated during analysis, because time and cost are both related and usually impact the cost of a project. Additionally, having independent personnel at the next higher management level to assess the analysis results to ascertain if they are optimistic, factual, or pessimistic is advocated as a form of due diligence to bring some assurance to the analysis step of the project control process. Many techniques and tools to support the analysis step are also suggested in the PCIM methodology. One of the most important techniques is the earned value analysis, which enables the integration of not just the cost and time as stated earlier but also scope. Other techniques for analysis recommended include cost–value reconciliation, S-curve, work breakdown structure (WBS), and cost breakdown structure (CBS). Finally, the use of modeling software packages was put forward by the PCIM project control methodology for use as part of the analysis stage of the project control process. For example, a good practice is modeling cost and time when analyzing using a 5-D model to visualize how the design develops (3-D), how time is being expended (4-D), and how the cost develops (5-D) based on the current trajectory data and information from the project.

Conclusion

Some 54 percent of the good practices that have been included in the PCIM project control methodology to support the project control steps have been rated by the Delphi experts as important during the PCIM project control methodology research. Some of these "important" good practices include ensuring there is a procurement strategy for buying all packages in the project at the tender stage; establishment of a structure within the project control process; aligning the cost breakdown structure with the work breakdown structure; specifying clearly what the deliverables of the project cost and time control will be to aid monitoring, and so on. Equally remarkable is the fact that some 29 percent of the good practices for the project control steps in the PCIM methodology were rated by the Delphi experts as critical to the relevant project control step. Some of these "critical" practices are obviously the life blood of the control process and it is little surprise that most of the expert panel within the Delphi process to determine the significance of the good practices of the PCIM project control methodology agreed that they were critical. Some of these critical practices include development of a schedule for the project time estimate; ensuring the project schedule is realistic; always monitoring the project time progress against the critical path; making sure the reporting is always honest and true, and so on. These practices are critical for an effective control of projects.

Some 17 percent of the good practices were determined by the Delphi experts as being helpful practices. These practices while not critical or considered important are useful good practices that should be embarked on during project control. None of the developed practices emerged as being unhelpful. This comes as no surprise because all the project control steps supporting practices put forward by the PCIM project control methodology are in fact good practices and were included in the list because they have been considered as having the potential to aid effective project cost, scope, and time control. Putting this in context, 83 percent of the good practices are considered as either critical or important in aiding project control and the remaining 17 percent were considered helpful. This high percentage of good practices Delphi rated as critical or important validates the practices and justifies the importance of having a good practice checklist to accompany the PCIM project control methodology. The significance attributed to these good practices would help to prioritize these good practices. This prioritization is useful so that, if for financial or other reasons, all the project control steps good practices contained in the PCIM project control methodology cannot be deployed by an organization during the project control process, then implementation should be in this order: good practices rated as critical, followed by the good practices rated as important, and then good practices rated as helpful.

PART 2

Classical Techniques Used During Project Control

CHAPTER 7

Classical Project Time Control Techniques

Overview

Although projects have been managed since the dawn of civilization, but the terms, concepts, and techniques of project management only began to be developed around 1910s when one of the most common project scheduling tools, the Gantt bar chart, was popularized. Since then, various techniques of project management have been developed, including many that are used for controlling the time of projects. In Chapter 6, the PCIM project control methodology put forward several of these project time control techniques to support the good practices contained in the PCIM project control methodology for the project control steps of planning, monitoring, reporting, and analyzing. The most common project time control techniques are explained in this chapter following a discussion on the concept of project time control below.

Project Time (Schedule) Control

The control of time is also often referred to as schedule control. This process involves determining the status of the project schedule, determining if changes have occurred or should, and implementing and managing schedule changes. It is important to apply time control on projects because, for the outcome of a project to be beneficial, it must be obtained within timescales and Turner (2006) argued that there are at least three ways in which time can have an impact:

- When the output only has the desired benefit at a certain time, for example a sporting event such as the 2022 men's football world cup in Qatar has a defined time at which the event must start, if the project is late all the benefit is lost.

- Sometimes the output of a project only has the desired benefit over a limited market window. An example could be the launch of a seasonal product.
- Due to the time value of money, the later a project is delivered the more it costs, and so value is eroded.

The Essential Element of Time Control: The Project Schedule

The project schedule is an essential prerequisite for time control of projects. It is one of the most important tools in the control of the time plan of a project. This is not surprising because first and foremost planning is an important technique of project management and the project schedule is an important project time planning tool. The master schedule for a project shows all the project stakeholders the start date and the completion time of a project (See section titled "Visual Representation of Project Duration" in chapter 3, for more information on different types of project schedules used in practice). The master schedule also details the important phases of work, their duration, and a breakdown of major work to be done during each stage. The project schedule is therefore an important measure of the progress being made in relation to the completion date during the delivery of the project. If used factually and accurately, analysis of the project schedule would show if the project is ahead of schedule, on schedule, or behind schedule. The project schedule can therefore be used to measure and control time progress, and if things were not going according to plan, the project team would need to find a remedy for the situation. The following sections discuss some key issues relating to the project schedule.

Description and Purpose of the Project Schedule

A schedule is the conversion of a project plan into the constituent activities with their associate completion timeline, which then creates a timetable upon aggregation. It is a series of dates against the elements in the work breakdown structure, which record when the project management team forecast the work will occur and, through monitoring, when the work eventually happens. The project schedule records the planned and actual start date, finish date, and duration of each work element. It may also record whether there is any flexibility when each element may start without delaying the completion of the project, which is called the float (discussed later in the chapter).

The aim of work scheduling is to achieve an economic balance between the utilization of resources and the cost of work in progress. This means that the scheduled time of a project is linked to the cost incurred as has been noted by the PCIM project control methodology. Scheduling work to be completed rapidly would usually have a high-cost implication due the use of additional resources or manhours than planned or working over-time, which will need to be paid for. While scheduling work to progress too slowly will usually also incur a higher cost due to spending more time in delivering the project. Therefore, the project schedule helps achieve the right balance based on the objectives of the project owner and available resources for the project. The project schedule helps to highlight the major elements of the time and progression plan of a project and communicate these to the stakeholders. The purposes of a project schedule are as follows:

- Presents the activities to be delivered on a project;
- Shows the sequence of the project activities;
- Includes the interdependencies of project activities;
- Includes the key project milestones;
- Shows key dates;
- Shows the milestone dates;
- Presents the operational approach and logic for delivering the project;
- Used to deliver the project;
- Provides a means of monitoring the progress of deliverables within the execution phase of the project;
- Serves as the basis for monitoring and controlling project activity.

Types of Schedule

The main approaches to scheduling are bar charts (Gantt charts), milestone charts, and networks such as arrow diagram method (ADM), precedence diagram method (PDM), program/graphical evaluation, and review techniques and linear scheduling such as line of balance (LOB) have been argued as an approach as well.

From the aforementioned, it is apparent that schedules can be classified broadly as non-network-based schedules and network-based schedules.

Non-Network-Based Schedules

These types of schedules include milestones and bar charts. The most popular non-network-based schedule is the bar chart or Gantt chart; it is one of the oldest and simplest forms of the project schedule. The Gantt chart was named after the famous management consultant Henry L. Gantt (1861–1919) (Seymour and Hussein 2014). Despite its age, the Gantt chart is still an important and popular tool in 21st century project management. The Gantt chart technique is discussed later in this chapter.

Network-Based Schedules

Network-based time control techniques sequence the activities required in the implementation of a project diagrammatically as a network showing the interdependencies and interrelationships of these activities. The planning data in the network is linked through the logic that defines the relationships between the activities. Therefore, changes can be made in the data relating to individual activities (i.e., the duration, the resources, etc.) or changes can be made in the logical relationships between activities and the consequences recalculated and represented.

Milestone Technique

One of the simplest techniques for controlling projects is the milestone technique. This is basically a time scheduling technique, which allows important deadlines in a project to be highlighted by specific points in time, called milestones. These activities are usually at the beginning or end of a phase or stage and are used for monitoring purposes throughout the life of the project. A milestone schedule will show the key events of a project (the milestones), on a diagrammatical representation of the project's delivery sequence forecast from start to finish. The key to helpful use of milestones techniques is selectivity, that is, choosing only a few key events as milestones. The disadvantage of the milestone technique is that it does not clarify the dependencies associated with activities or tasks.

Milestone Slip Chart

A milestone slip chart is a type of progress report as shown in Figure 7.1. For projects, it can be developed by plotting the milestones associated with a project on a grid on a periodic basis to indicate the planned date for that milestone.

How the milestone slip chart is used in practice is described below.

- Week "0": In Figure 7.1, the start of the project is a point "0." In the baseline schedule, milestone A is due to occur in week 2, milestone B in week 5, and milestone C in week 7.
- Week 1: After the first week, the three milestones, A, B, and C are on track.
- Week 2: However, by the end of week two, they have fallen behind their planned date by one week.
- Week 3: At the end of week three, A is completed but one week later than planned and the other milestones are still behind their planned date by one week.

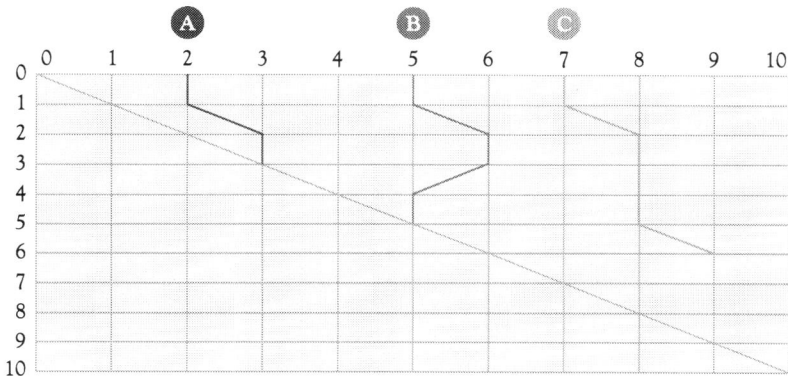

Figure 7.1 Example of a milestone slip chart

- Week 4: In week four, B is back on track but C is still behind its planned date by one week.
- Week 5: In week five, B is completed on time.
- Week 6: However, in week six, C is now behind its planned date by an additional week.

The advantage of the milestone slip chart is its simplicity and ability to present a high-level view of progress using the key milestones dates of the project transferred from the detailed project schedule.

Graphical Analysis (Bar Charts)

Bar charts as previously mentioned are often called Gantt charts after Henry Laurence Gantt, an American engineer and management consultant who popularized them during the First World War. During this period, Gantt worked with the U.S. Army on a method for visually portraying the status of the munitions' programs. He realized that time was common denominator to most elements of a project's delivery schedule and that progress could easily be assessed by viewing each element's status with respect to time (Nicholas 2020).

Although the bar charts are popularly named after Gantt, it was Karol Adamiecki, a Polish engineer and economist researcher who first developed a novel means of displaying interdependent processes to enhance the visibility of production schedules in 1896. However, his works were published in Polish and Russian languages and were not popular in the English-speaking world where Gantt published on a similar technique in 1910 and 1915. Therefore, this technique is referred to in English by Gantt's name. Gantt charts were utilized in many major American First World War infrastructure projects including the Hoover Dam, which as concluded by Seymour and Hussein (2014), popularized it and contributed to its widespread adoption. Figure 7.2 shows an example of a bar chart used to schedule a project. The structure of the Gantt chart is as follows:

- A horizontal timescale to show activity duration
- A vertical list of activities
- A horizontal line or bar for each activity

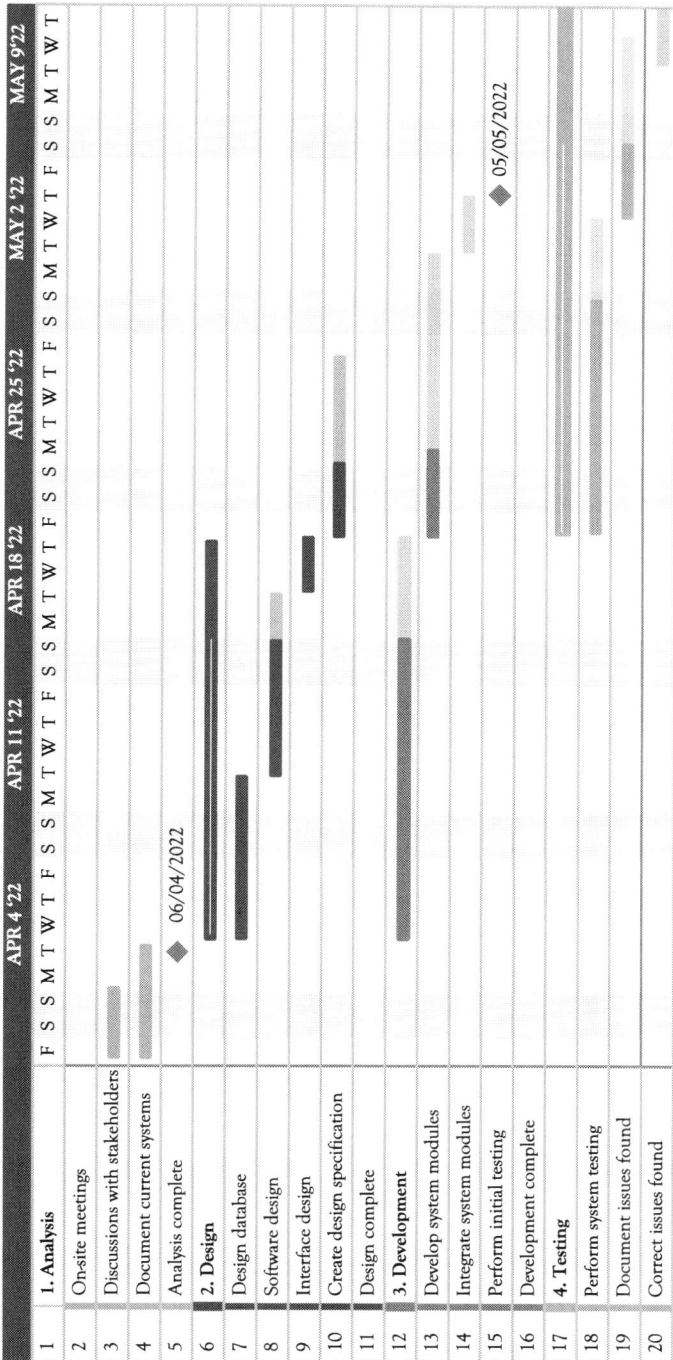

Figure 7.2 Example of a bar chart

In addition to these, bar charts show the sequence of activities to be delivered on a project graphically using the dependencies and interrelationship between or among activities. They can also show schedule dates, milestones, key dates, and can be used to show current progress status of the project.

Advantages of Bar Charts

- Bar charts are easy to develop for projects and update as the project progresses.
- They can be used to provide a high-level overview of a project's timetable including dependencies and overlaps.
- Stakeholders find them more straightforward to understand.
- They can be used to present the timelines of multiple projects in a noncomplex format, then used to monitor and control the progress of the multiple projects.
- The critical path is produced before the floats are known unlike some other methods, where the floats must be calculated first before the critical path can be seen. The advantage of this is that the scheduler or planner can know immediately whether the project time is within the specified limits and adjust the critical activities without bothering with the noncritical ones (Lester 2017).

Limitations of Bar Charts

- One of the disadvantages of the Gantt chart, according to Nicholas (2020), is that it does not show explicitly the interrelationships among work elements, that is, it does not reveal the effect of one work element falling behind schedule on other elements.
- Bar charts provide only a vague description of how the entire program or project reacts as a system; they do not show the interdependencies of the activities and therefore do not represent a "network" of activities. Since the relationship between activities is crucial for controlling project costs, bar charts have little predictive value (Kerzner (2017).

- Knowing the status of project activities gives no information at all about overall project status because only one activity's dependence on another is shown.
- Bar charts are often maintained manually. This is usually not a problem for small projects but onerous for large projects, consequently causing lethargic updates and results in the bar charts becoming outdated.
- Bar charts, according to Kerzner (2017), do not show the uncertainty involved in performing each activity and, therefore, do not lend themselves readily to sensitivity analysis. For instance, answering questions like: What is the shortest time or longest time an activity might take? What is the average or expected time to complete an activity?
- The use of percentage completion mostly used for progress monitoring on bar charts usually leads to subjectivity and confusion as it does not provide the information on whether the performance dimension relates to the schedule dimension or the cost dimension. Therefore, it becomes impossible to judge what percentage of activity is truly complete.

LOB Method

The LOB method originated in the Goodyear Company in the 1940s and was developed by the U.S. Navy during the Second World War. The method is used when a project consists of blocks of the same or similar work or repetitive activities. It is often used where the same activities are performed by the same team; hence it is also referred to as the linear scheduling method. The LOB (See Figure 7.3) compares time and location or sequence number of repetitive elements. The horizontal axis plots time, while the vertical axis plots location or distance along the length of a project. Individual activities are plotted separately, resulting in a series of diagonal lines. The slopes of the diagonal lines represent the planned rate of progress at any time of any activity. The completion time for each activity is a function of the rate of progress and the amount of work to be undertaken.

The production goal is determined by the scope of the project. Based on the requirements of the users, the delivery schedule is produced; thereafter the production goal can be expressed in terms of the objective chart. The time required to produce the unit is calculated and the completion times and lead times of each activity are determined after which the progress chart is drawn. The horizontal scale corresponds to the number of control points in the production plan. The vertical scale corresponds to the cumulative quantities of the production units. The LOB is the level of the cumulative qualities, which must be available at any specific delivery time. The basis of the technique, as noted by Harris, McCaffer, and Edum-Fotwe (2013), is to find the required resources for each stage or operation so that the subsequent stages are not interfered with while achieving the target output.

Advantages and Disadvantages of the LOB Method

As would have been noted earlier, the main advantage of using the LOB is that it is a very useful control technique that can be used for repetitive projects, which means it may be unsuitable for nonrepetitive projects. Scheduling techniques utilizing network analysis are usually employed for planning one-off projects, be it a construction project, a manufacturing operation, a computer software development, or a move to new premises. However, when the overall project consists of several identical operations,

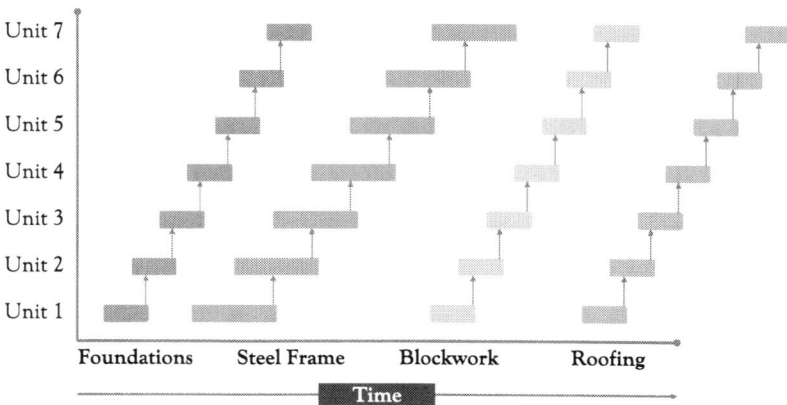

Figure 7.3 Example of a LOB chart

each of which may be a subproject, then the use of the LOB technique may be advantageous. In addition to this, the advantages and disadvantages of the LOB technique include the following.

Advantages

- It is a simple process that can be implemented manually.
- It provides a graphical interface that enables users to identify and interpret the production rates, durations, and relationships between repeating tasks quickly (Tokdemir, Erol, and Dikmen 2019).
- Each line on a LOB shows the rate of progress of an activity, which neither bar charts nor network schedules can do.
- It presents clearly the quantity of work taking place in certain areas and at a specific time of the project.
- It serves as a midway between bar charts and networks from a complexity viewpoint. Therefore, the LOB is easier to develop than a network schedule, but it is more rigorous than a bar chart.
- It facilitates the incorporation of the learning effect during scheduling, which results in a gradual reduction in the labor-hours requirements of repeating tasks (Tokdemir et al. 2019).
- It can also be used for nonrepetitive activities, especially when there is a need to evaluate the best combination of individual progress rates.

Disadvantages

- The disadvantages include the disadvantage associated with non-network-based techniques such as the bar chart as described in the section titled Non-Network-Based Schedules" earlier in this chapter.
- A major difficulty in LOB is determining the buffer interval (the buffer is the duration by which an activity could be delayed without affecting the overall project duration), which sometimes can best be found out when the production rates of adjacent activities are known.

- Updating the LOB once a project has started can be difficult and become quickly unclear, especially if the actual rates of construction prove to be different from those planned (Harris, McCaffer, and Edum-Fotwe, 2013).

Precedence Diagramming Method

The precedence diagramming method (PDM) grew out of the arrow networks to overcome some of the arrow network faults. In the PDM, three different notations are available to show a variety of start-to-finish relationships to fit any type of activity. This gives more flexibility to notation when developing logic diagrams. The PDM shows the activity number in the block, which then leaves more room to describe the activity in greater detail.

The PDM allows the overall project to be presented visually as a precedence diagram, known as the overall precedence. It can also be used to show part of the project to create partial precedence diagrams. A precedence diagram is created using graphical methods. The most visually imposing part of a PDM is the node. The node describes the connection point and an arrow of a presentation element to indicate the relationship between two nodes. The PDM (See Figure 7.4) is made up of processes (activities with established earliest and latest start and end points), event (defined and documented state in a project), and relationship (dependencies between individual processes).

Advantages of PDM

- The arrow network scheduling procedures assume a strict sequential relationship upon which the start of an activity is predicated upon the completion of its immediate predecessors, that is, a finish-to-start (FS) relationship. However, the PDM is not this strict and can handle the scheduling of tasks that can start when their predecessors are completed partially (but not fully).
- Besides the usual FS relationships, PDM permits the relationships of start-to-start, finish-to-finish, and start-to-finish and has the ability to show when an activity can start before the preceding one is completed.

2	Activity A		4	Activity C
0	0	0	5	0	0

1	Start
0	0	0

5	Finish
0	0	0

3	Activity B
4	2	2

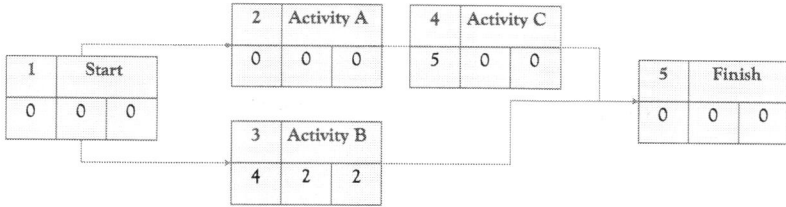

Figure 7.4 Example of a precedence diagram

- The PDM allows dependencies between activities and the effects of changes to be quickly recognized.
- It helps in the identification of relationships and dependencies among activities to identify easily any missing task.
- It allows the identification of critical processes and activities, which can then be presented as a critical path.

Limitations of PDM

The drawbacks of the PDM are as follows:

- First, because of the lead and lag requirement, activities may appear to have a float when they really do not.
- Second, as highlighted by Meredith, Shafer, and Mantel (2021), it is susceptible to reverser critical phenomenon where the critical path enters the completion of an activity through a finish constraint, continues backward through the activity, and leaves through a start constraint. The consequence of this is that increasing an activity time may actually decrease the project completion time inadvertently.

Critical Path Method

The critical path method (CPM) was almost simultaneously developed in 1958 by the Central Electric Generating Board in England and the joint effort of the U.S. Navy and one of its contractors (Du Pont) in the United States (Lester 2017). CPM includes a mathematical procedure for estimating the trade-off between project duration and project cost and, as asserted by Nicholas (2020), the CPM features the analysis of

Early start	Duration	Early finish
Task name		
Late start	Float	Late finish

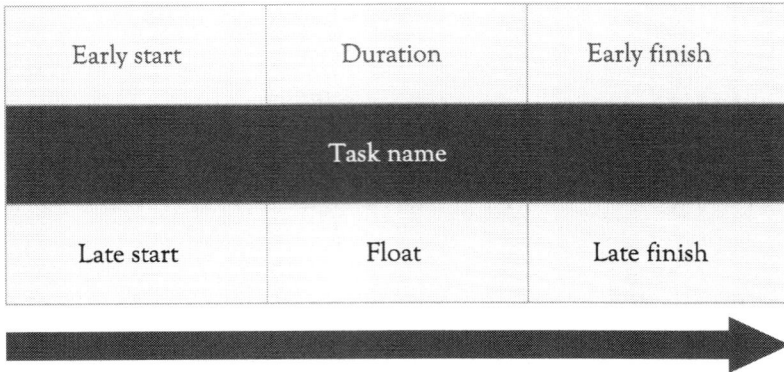

Figure 7.5 Node and arrow in a CPM network

reallocation of resources from one job to another to achieve the greatest reduction in project duration at the least cost. The fundamental purpose of CPM is to enable the identification of the minimum overall project duration. The critical path of a project is the longest duration logically required to complete a project; with any delay in activities on this critical path will delay the completion date of the project. It is the path where all the activities on it have zero float (float is the amount of time an activity can be delayed before it begins to delay the project; it is the amount of time between the completion of an activity and its succeeding activity). The relationships between activities in a critical path are shown using networks. A network typically contains the nodes that contain information about the activities and arrows that are used to show the logical relationships between activities such as finish-to-start, start-to-start, finish-to-finish (see Figure 7.5).

Uses and Advantages of the CPM

- The CPM has been used widely for project scheduling, helping managers to guarantee the timely and on-budget completion of projects by identifying the most critical elements of the project.
- CPM shows the activities and their outcomes as a network diagram and enables the identification of activities that can be delivered simultaneously.

- CPM provides useful information for the project, such as the critical path(s) and free and total float, which are essential for the efficient planning of a project.
- It can aid in the optimization of the project through the determination of the overall project duration.
- It can facilitate management by exceptions through a focus on critical and near-critical activities, especially on projects that are large and complex.
- CPM establishes the dependencies among activities of a project and aids the scheduling of individual activities.

Limitations of CPM

- CPM assumes that there are unlimited resources for the execution of the activities, but in real projects, resources are not unlimited. Thus, scheduling without considering resource constraints gives unreliable schedules.
- Because the CPM caters to the scheduling of resource allocation, it is not suitable for scheduling resource-constrained projects.
- The critical path is not always clear and it can sometimes be difficult to estimate the activity completion time in a multidimensional project.
- Identifying and determining a critical path can be difficult when there are many other similar duration paths in the project.
- The CPM network can become very complicated on big projects and not straightforward for all project stakeholders to comprehend.
- The critical path needs to be always calculated accurately, therefore requiring a lot of time and effort; for big projects with long durations, it requires the use of software to monitor the schedule.
- CPM can become ineffective and difficult to manage if it is not well-defined and stable.

- Sudden changes in the delivery plan of the project during execution can be problematic when using the CPM, that is, it can be challenging to redraw the entire CPM chart if the plan of the project suddenly deviates from the original.

Program Evaluation and Review Technique

The program evaluation and review technique (PERT) was originally developed in 1958 to meet the needs of the "age of massive engineering" where the techniques of Gantt were not sophisticated sufficiently. The Special Projects Office of the U.S. Navy, concerned with performance trends on large military development program, introduced PERT on its Polaris Weapon System in 1958. According to Kezner (2017), this was after the technique had been developed with the aid of the management consulting firm of Booz, Allen, and Hamilton as a way of handling uncertainties in the estimating activity times. PERT has since spread rapidly throughout almost all industries. It adopts the critical path like the CPM described earlier to compute expected project duration, early and late times, and floats. Although, as highlighted by Nicholas (2020), PERT and CPM are similar, they were developed independently in different problem environments and industries. PERT is event-oriented (i.e., the event labels go in the nodes of the diagram) and has typically been used in aerospace and research development projects for which the time for each activity is uncertain. PERT is mostly applied to projects characterized by uncertainties; therefore, its focus is probabilistic and applies statistical treatment to the possible range of activity time duration as described in the section below.

PERT Time Estimating

PERT networks originated in projects characterized by uncertain times for activities as noted above. This problem of uncertain times was dealt with by requiring three-point probabilistic time estimates for each activity, that is:

- The most likely activity time;
- The optimistic activity time, which is the shortest time that might be achieved 1 percent of the time such an activity was carried out;

- The pessimistic activity time, which is, the longest time that would be exceeded only 1 percent of the time such an activity was carried out.

The range between the estimates provides a measure of variability, which permits statistical inferences to be made about the likelihood of project events happening at a time (Nicholas 2020). This procedure differentiates PERT from the CPM, which calculates the critical path and slack times (float) only using best estimates of activities. As shown in Figure 7.6, the three estimates are related in the form of a beta probability distribution with parameters O (optimistic time) and P (pessimistic time) as the end points, and M (most likely time) the most frequent value. The beta distribution was chosen by the originators because it is unimodal, has finite end points, and is not necessarily symmetrical, properties that seem desirable for a distribution time. Based on this distribution, the mean or expected time (t_e) and variance (V) of each activity are computed with three estimates of time as below:

$$t_e = (O + 4M + P)/6 \qquad (7.1)$$

$$V = ((P - O)/6)^2 \qquad (7.2)$$

It is important to point out that the above formulas are shortcuts and a simplistic view. A more rigorous approach involves probabilistic

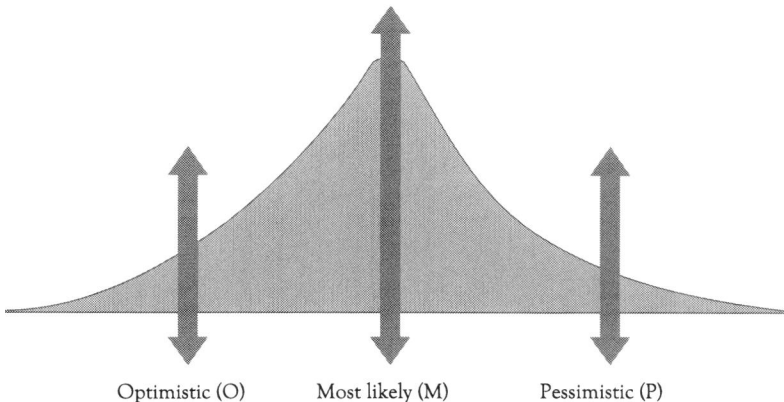

Optimistic (O)   Most likely (M)   Pessimistic (P)

Figure 7.6 PERT distribution curve

simulation using computer simulations such as Monte Carlo simulation, which can be found in most statistical books.

Advantages and Disadvantages of PERT

The advantages and disadvantages of PERT are as follows.

Advantages

- Interdependencies and problem areas that may not be obvious by other scheduling methods become obvious quickly due to the kind of detailed planning required to create the PERT network.
- The PERT method usually shows the critical path in an organized diagram and well-defined manner, therefore helping the project manager and other stakeholders to make quick and quality decisions to the benefit of the project.
- It enables "what if" analysis to be carried out on projects, that is, the effect of changes in the schedule, which helps identify the risks associated with activities. The possibilities and the various level of uncertainties can then be studied from the project activities by analyzing the critical path properly, enabling the most suitable combination (minimum cost, economy, and best result) to be chosen for the project.
- It enables the determination of the probability of meeting specified deadlines by development of alternatives plans since statistical analysis such as standard deviations can be utilized with it.
- The activities and the events from the PERT networks can be analyzed independently as well as in combination to provide a picture of the likely completion of the project and the associated budget.

Disadvantages

- One of the greatest disadvantages of PERT is that it can be very complex, making it time- and labor-intensive to operate.

- Additionally, due to a large data requirement, PERT is an expensive technique to maintain and is therefore mostly used in large complex projects and not in day-to-day management of smaller projects.
- The activities for a project are identified based on available data, but finding data for new or nonrepetitive projects is often difficult, leading to the use of subjective, biased, or unreliable information, which could lead to inaccurate estimated time.
- Predictions are often used to develop the PERT time, which could lead to the overall project achieving budget loss if the predictions and the decisions are inaccurate.
- PERT also has the disadvantage that it may result in a lack of functional ownership in estimates and assumes unlimited resources. However, this is usually not the case.
- The PERT method is reliant on estimation of different times to complete activities; therefore, it is not useful when no reasonable estimates of time can be made.

Graphical Evaluation and Review Technique

The graphical evaluation and review technique (GERT) is similar to PERT, but, as pointed out by Nicholas (2020), it has the distinct advantages of allowing for looping, branching, and multiple project end results. For example, with PERT, it cannot be easily shown that if an activity is unsuccessful; it may have to be repeated several times and one of several different branches can only be selected to continue the project. However, this challenge is easily overcome using GERT.

PDM, PERT, and CPM are limited as tools in their capacity to model a project realistically because of the following limitations as highlighted by Nicholas (2020):

- All immediate predecessor activities must be completed before a given activity can be started.
- No activity can be repeated, and no looping back to predecessors is permitted.

- The duration time for an activity is restricted to the beta distribution for PERT and a single estimate (deterministic) for CPM.
- The critical path is always considered the longest path even though variances include the likelihood of other paths being longer.
- There is only one terminal event and the only way to reach it is by completing all activities in the project.

The GERT technique overcomes these limitations as it permits alternative time distribution and allows looping back so that previous activities can be repeated as previously mentioned. The major distinction of GERT is that it utilizes complex nodes. In PERT, a node is an event that represents the start or finish of an activity and cannot be realized until all its immediate predecessors have been realized. GERT utilizes probabilistic and branching nodes that specify both the number of activities leading to them that must be realized as well as the potential multiple branching paths that can emanate from them.

Table 7.1 presents a summary of the differences that exist between the GERT and the CPM/PERT techniques as asserted by Meredith, Shafer, and Mantel (2021).

An Appraisal of the Suitability of the Time Control Techniques

The previous sections have presented most of the prevalent/classical project time control techniques that can be used for projects.

It could be noted from the Table 7.2 that quite often the project time control techniques have their own strengths and weaknesses. Therefore, for project time control, there is no one-cap-fits-all technique. For example, traditionally, the time control of the duration of projects has been carried out most frequently by means of Gantt charts. The problem with the Gantt bar chart is that it may not be effective for project time control. Some of the reasons for this were indicated in the weaknesses. First, the bar chart—although well known, simple, cheap to use, and familiar as a means of communication—has the following disadvantages: planning

Table 7.1 Differences between GERT and PERT/CPM

	GERT	PERT/CPM
1	Branching from a node is probabilistic	Branching from a node is deterministic
2	Various possible probability	Only the beta distribution for time estimates
3	Flexibility in node realization	No flexibility in node realization
4	Looping back to earlier events is acceptable	Looping back is not allowed
5	Difficult to use as a control tool	Easy to use as a control tool
6	Arc may represent time, cost, reliability, etc.	Arc represents time only

and scheduling must be carried out at one and the same time as the bars are constructed; dependencies of one operation or activity on others are not shown; control is restricted to that of duration, and it is not easy to connect the physical quantities of work involved in each operation with specific period. Therefore, the time progress does not necessarily give an accurate indication of the actual physical progress of the work.

It was discussed that the category of planning and scheduling methods that overcomes many of the disadvantages of the bar chart is that of network analysis. As mentioned in this chapter, network analysis covers a range of techniques; the most popular ones are CPM, PERT, and PDM. Network analysis methods, when used for time control of projects, were shown as having many advantages such as providing a systematic approach to planning; enabling modeling to test various project delivery options before the start of work; making possible the true effect of changes to a project to be analyzed insofar as the changes affect other activities; and depicting clearly the interrelationships between the activities of the project. They reveal interdependencies of activities; they facilitate "what if" exercises; they identify the longest path or critical paths; they aid in scheduling risk analysis (Kerzner 2017).

However, despite this overwhelming list of advantages, network methods of project control have been criticized since their inception, for example, by Nicholas (2020) for the following reasons: they incorporate assumptions and yield results that sometimes are unrealistic or pose problems to their users; network methods assume that a project can be

Table 7.2 Trait summary of existing project cost and time control techniques

Technique	Applicability	Strengths	Weaknesses
Milestone date programming	Scheduling and time control	• Simple to use and selectivity of a few key events	• The technique does not clarify the activity of task interdependencies.
Graphical analysis (Bar chart)	Scheduling and time control	• Cheap and easy to use • Understood readily by most stakeholders	• Does not show explicitly interrelationships and dependencies among work elements • Does not show the uncertainty involved in performing an activity • Control is restricted to duration (time) only. • Not easy to connect the physical quantities of work involved in each operation with a specific period. • Not easy to connect the physical quantities of work involved in each operation with a specific period. Therefore, the time progress does not necessarily give an accurate indication of the actual physical progress of the work.
LOB	Scheduling and time control	• Very useful for repetitive projects. • Provides more information than a bar chart. • Can be used to indicate the rate of progress of an activity • Conveys detailed work schedule simply	• Does not show explicitly the interrelationships among work elements • Does not show the uncertainty involved in performing an activity • Can become difficult and unclear quickly as a result of updating when a project has started
CPM	Scheduling and time control	• Provides very useful information about the project such as critical path(s) and free and total float necessary for efficient planning • Allows management by exceptions (critical and near-critical activities)	• Because the CPM assumes unlimited resources, which might give unreliable schedules for resource, constrained projects.

		Advantages	Disadvantages
PDM	Scheduling and time control	• Not limited by only finish-to-start or start-to-finish relationships as it allows other for other relationships such as start-to-start, finish-to-finish, and start-to-finish	• Because of the lead and lag requirements activities may appear to have slack when they really do not.
PERT	Scheduling and time control	• Quickly reveals interdependencies and problem areas that may not be obvious by other planning methods hence it determines where the greatest effort should be made for a project to stay on schedule. • Lends itself to statistical analysis and enables the determination of the probability of meeting specified deadlines by development of alternatives. • Has the ability to be used for the evaluation of the effect of changes in the program.	• Its complexity makes it difficult to implement. • Large data requirement makes it expensive to maintain and is therefore mostly used in large complex projects and not on day-to-day smaller projects. • May result in a lack of functional ownership in estimates and assumes unlimited resources, which is not always the case.
GERT	Scheduling and time control	• Allows for looping, branching, and multiple project end results. • Permits the use of probabilistic and branching nodes that specify both the number of activities, leading to them as well as the potential for multiple branching paths that can emanate from them (flexibility in node realization).	• It is difficult to use as a control tool because it may be complex.

completely defined as a sequence of identifiable, independent activities with known precedence relationships. In many projects, however, the work cannot be always anticipated, and not all activities can be clearly defined. Rather, projects evolve as they progress; it is difficult to demarcate one activity from the next, and the point of separation is arbitrary. Although the PDM helps overcome this difficulty in demarcating activities, precedence relationships are not always fixed with the start of one activity sometimes contingent upon the outcome of an earlier one, which may have to be repeated. The GERT method deals somewhat with this problem. Despite these disadvantages of network scheduling methods, it is important to note that network methods, though not perfect, are still the most helpful for project scheduling and time control and getting the best schedule estimate possible.

CHAPTER 8

Classical Project Cost Control Techniques

Overview

There are many techniques that have been developed for project cost control. This chapter presents the most common and relevant of these techniques. Cost control can be defined as the judicious utilization and safeguarding of the cost of carrying out various activities of a project or a contract by management. The focus of cost control is to make sure that all the activities of a project are completed within their budget estimate. Cost control involves the implementation of regular and up-to-date monitoring system (using various techniques). This, according to Lester (2017), enables the identification of the expenditure with specific operations or stages, determining whether the expenditure was cost effective, analyze trends, and then take immediate action if the trend is unacceptable. For most projects, the monitoring and control of costs is essential from the point of view of the key stakeholders such as the project owner, designers, contractor, subcontractors, and so on. In essence, apart from ensuring that projects are completed on time, managers are next concerned about cost because, save for exceptional cases, there is little consolation in finishing on time but at an escalated cost.

Project cost control begins with a preparation of the original cost estimate and the subsequent cost budget. Keeping the delivery of the project within the cost budget and knowing when and where job costs are deviating are two factors that constitute the key to successful delivery of a project from a financial perspective. Furthermore, cost control involves applying cost accounting methods to determine the actual costs of production by comparing the expended costs with the budget. In addition to monitoring the current project spend, periodic reports are prepared to forecast cost at completion and an estimate to complete (final project cost), which is then compared with the baseline budget to ascertain whether there will be a cost overrun.

Purpose of Project Cost Control

The ultimate objective of cost control in management is the execution of an operation in the most cost-efficient way possible. In a project environment, the objective of project cost control is to forecast the project cost at completion during the delivery of the project and identify any negative trends and deviations from the baseline budget to facilitate corrective measures to be taken. Therefore, cost control provides information to the project team about inefficient areas of the project including the data that can be used to compute any variance from the planned cost performance standards. Cost control according to the APM (2015) is also necessary to keep a record of monetary expenditure for purposes such as minimizing cost where possible; revealing areas of cost overspend; and using cost information for the lessons learned process to provide a database of actual costs against activities and work packages that can be used to inform future projects.

Profit and Loss System

The approach of using the profit and loss on a project or contract has been used as a form of cost control mechanism. There are two ways this approach is implemented in practice; these are described in the next two sections.

Overall Profit or Loss

The overall profit and loss of a project, although not a proactive cost control mechanism for current projects, can be used as a feedback cost control for future projects in an organization. The measure is used in project delivery contracting organizations, consulting companies, and similar organizations. In this system, management waits until the project is complete and then compares cost incurred in delivering the project for a client with the revenue received from the client for that project to ascertain the profit or loss made in executing the project. The analysis of areas where profit or loss were made should be carried out for lessons learned. This calculation of profit or loss only serves to prevent errors from happening in future projects as the information produced cannot be used for the current project. This form of cost control should be adopted at the end of every project. However, it should not be relied on as the only cost control mechanism for ongoing projects due to its retrospective nature.

Profit or Loss on Each Contract or Work Package at Valuation Dates

This system is slightly more proactive than the overall profit and loss approach. Here the total costs to date of packages of a contract or project are compared with valuations at a specific date, usually at the end of the month. Other costs incurred in relation to each work package or subcontract but not yet invoiced, such as cost of materials delivered but not yet invoiced by the supplier, are normally included. The money due to be paid for each work package at that specific date is then compared to the cost incurred for that work package to ascertain if each of the package is in loss or profit compared to the budget. This can help identify areas of the project that are currently experiencing overspends and need attention and require their cost to be controlled. The downside to this system is that there is no breakdown of the profit figure between types of work making up the section or contract of a project. Therefore, as noted by Harris et al. (2013), it only shows which subcontract or work package requires attention and does not show it to the level of activities making up the work package.

Unit and Standard Costing

Unit Costing

A unit cost is the total expenditure involved in creating one unit of a product or service. In this system of cost control, costs of various types of work in the project are recorded separately. At the outset during cost estimation, the project is divided into various components. The cost of each of the project's components is then calculated, and these costs are summed up to arrive at the overall project cost. As the project progresses, the costs both cumulatively and on a periodic basis are divided by the quantity of work of each type of work that has been done. This provides the actual unit costs that can be compared with those in the initial estimate for the project at the outset to indicate where the unit costs during execution of the project are higher, lower, or as estimated. Any necessary action can then be taken to control costs higher than estimates or budgets. It is usually best to record and compare project-level costs only, net of profit and overheads. The advantages of unit costing include the fact that it is simple and quick to implement. However, because it divides the cost extended on a quantity of work by the quantity of work for each type of work without context, it has the drawback of being unreliable and producing large deviations from the actual cost incurred.

Standard Costing

Standard costing involves the creation of estimated costs (the standard costs) for some or all activities within a company and by so doing its projects. The core reason for using standard costs is that it may be challenging to collect actual costs for all the activities in a company, so standard costs are used as a close approximation to actual costs. To control costs during implementation of a project, variances are calculated by comparing the value of the output with the cost of producing it. A variance is the amount by which the achieved profit differs from the budgeted profit, and this is analyzed into subvariances such as material price, material usage, labor rate, labor efficiency, fixed and variable overhead expenditure, volume of production, sales, and so on. This system provides comprehensive cost control for the company from boardroom down to workforce. However, a key limitation of this method is its lack of suitability for cost-plus contracts where actual costs are required, as per the terms of the contract. It is also not suitable in a fast-paced environment because the assumption that comes with standard costing is that costs do not change much in the near term and are usually not updated frequently. Therefore, standard costs are susceptible to being out-of-date in a fast-paced environment.

PERT/Cost System

Program evaluation review technique (PERT)/Cost was developed in 1962 when the U.S. Air Force came up with an extension of PERT by adding resource estimates to the logic networks. Fleming and Koppelman (1998) noted that PERT/Cost relates to the value of physical work performed against the cost actuals to determine the utility and benefits from the funds spent. It is a PERT-based system (see Chapter 7 for a discussion of the PERT technique), which combines cost with scheduling. In the system, cost classifications are based upon project work breakdowns so that costs can be identified with the activities on the PERT network. The breakdowns serve as vehicles for both estimating and accumulating costs, thus PERT/Cost can be utilized to control the cost of projects. PERT/Cost employs the same principle used to produce the three-point probabilistic estimate for time in PERT as described in Chapter 7 to estimate ranges for cost instead of duration. In the PERT/Cost technique, the most likely cost estimate, the most optimistic cost estimate, and the most pessimistic cost estimate are used to calculate a mean cost for each of the activities of a project. The mean cost of all the activities added together will produce the mean total project cost.

Advantages and Limitations of PERT/Cost

PERT/Cost is a major improvement over traditional cost accounting techniques because it blends costs with work schedules. PERT/Cost was the original network-based project cost accounting system (PCAS). Most PCASs integrate work packages, cost accounts, and project schedules into a unified project control package. They permit cost and scheduling overruns to be identified and causes to be quickly pinpointed among numerous work packages and cost accounts (Nicholas 2020). The limitation of this technique is that it cannot be applied directly where the work is valued by a bill of quantities, which relates to the complete work rather than the operation (Harris et al. 2013). It is more useful in design and build project where the contractor can provide a valuation document that shows the operations to be performed (an activities schedule) because

PERT/Cost requires an activity or operational schedule instead of the normal bill of quantities. Additionally, while the PERT/Cost technique provides a substantial measure of cost control for large complex projects, the breaking up of large projects into smaller more manageable units may increase the overall problem of coordination in managing costs on projects. Cost estimates in PERT/Cost may also eventually end up as budgets, and even though cost estimates are subject to revision, there is a tendency to inflate the budget in the initial planning stage.

Cost Value Reconciliation

Cost value reconciliation (CVR) is the comparison of the project value with the project cost at predetermined periodic interval during the progress of a project. This interval is normally monthly and tends to tie in with the company's valuation and accounting procedures. The CVR process allows management and statutory procedures accounts to be prepared on a more meaningful basis. The CVRs are usually completed by the cost personnel on the project such as a quantity surveyor or cost engineer on construction and engineering projects. However, they are produced in liaison with other departments, for example, operations, project management delivery, procurement, accounting, and so on.

The reason for CVRs, especially in construction and civil engineering contracting companies, is first and foremost to monitor and therefore control the overall project. The CVR process allows the monitoring of the performance of a project in terms of cost of labor, plant and machinery usage, material cost against the budget figures, and taking control action if necessary. The CVR process also facilitates the comparison of the overall project profitability against budget and forecasts. It is also a good management practice utilized by construction and civil engineering contracting companies to provide overall accounting information to management and helps to satisfy accounting standards that prescribe the accounting treatment of revenue and cost associated with construction project contracts. Examples of such accounting standards include International Financial Reporting Standards (IFRS) 15 (revenue from contracts with customer) that replaced Internal Accounting Standards (IAS) 11 (construction contracts) in January 2018.

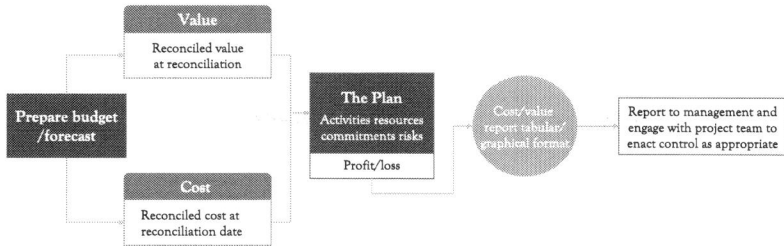

Figure 8.1 Principles of cost value reconciliation

Figure 8.1 depicts the CVR process, which indicates that there are two important aspects of a project that need to be understood in producing CVRs. These are as follows:

- The current cost expended for that value of work including liabilities to third parties and suppliers related to the work
- The current value of work

Cost Reconciliation in CVR

Costs are normally produced for each project monthly and will usually indicate accurately the amount of money spent. The cost should include items such as invoices, salaries as well as liabilities for work done that is yet to be invoiced by the third party or supplier. If these liabilities are not taken into account, then the cost reported for the month will indicate a false position. The liability will need to be recognized and added to the "paid" cost position (this is what is called a cost accrual). Many companies' financial statements are prepared under the accrual basis of accounting where revenue and costs are recognized when earned (work carried out or service performed) and incurred respectively. Accruals are made for costs that have arisen for activities prior to the reporting date. Therefore, all goods and services received within the reporting period should be accrued for, if not already costed to the contract automatically through the company's financial system.

Most projects will have their costs grouped against major headings. These are further divided into a series of subheadings to enable closer scrutiny of aspects of the job. The cost allocation must be true and accurate each month, as the monthly reports are used continuously by management to monitor not only the performance of the project, but other areas as well, such as the company's profit margin, liabilities, cashflow, and so on. The regular monitoring of costs helps to determine whether the project is being delivered as planned or has gone off course, in which case the CVR reporting will highlight areas for appropriate corrective action to be taken.

Value Reconciliation in CVR

Value is what is earned from doing the work, and it is the quantity of work multiplied by the rate for doing the work, that is, the "agreed price," not the "cost" of doing the work. That is, value is equal to net cost, plus overheads and profit. In the reporting of value during the CVR process, the concern is about the true "earned" (or internal) value of the work done and any out of balance recovery must be taken into consideration before reporting the contract position at any point in time. Without this adjustment, either an overstatement or understatement of the actual position will be given. Consequently, the external valuation (i.e., that certified by the client) may need to be adjusted to reflect appropriately the true earned value of the work carried out (See Table 8.1 for CVR good practices).

Advantages and Limitations of CVRs

Advantages:

- The CVR can be useful in comparing the current profitability and turnover of a project against what was estimated in the budget as well as the forward forecast.
- The CVR can be used to monitor project performance in terms of labor, plant, and material cost against original tender information, which can then be used to minimize overspending and control cost.
- The CVR can be used to facilitate increased accuracy of pricing of future projects since it provides information on general

performance that can be used when assessing tenders on other similar projects.

- Once projects commence, cost value comparison is normally carried out on a monthly basis and the results of each project are then monitored against the anticipated performance, which provides management information that can help in the identification of problems on projects.
- CVRs can provide information that can aid cash management especially on large projects and the organization.
- CVRs provides organizations with the ability to control the project from outside the boundary of the project, due to CVR cost control measures being applied at the organizational level to achieve the desired project performance to meet the organizational objectives.

Table 8.1 CVR good practices

1. In reporting cost and value at monthly or other regular frequencies, the objective is usually to report the true position at that point in respect of cost incurred and income earned and to reconcile this with the overall prediction of the outturn profitability for the project.
2. Cost and value reporting and reconciliation is not simply a case of adding up invoices paid to determine cost.
3. Equally, it is not a matter of simply adding up the payment received to determine the earned value.
4. To obtain a true reflection of the position at any point, the adjustments must be made to both the cost and value sides of the equation.
5. Value should only be taken when it is secure and not liable to reduction in the future.
6. Value is taken against both completed and work in progress (both certified and not certified by the client), but only to a value where it is not likely to be reduced.
7. All costs relative to the value taken are recorded within the CVR.
8. Accruals for costs that have been incurred but not recorded on the system are accrued for in the CVR.
9. A key component of the CVR is the recognition of the true liability to subcontractors and suppliers.
10. It is important to recognize that the true liability to each subcontractor is not solely the amount paid, but it is the realistic financial obligation to the subcontractor at the reporting date or if the subcontractor stops trading, what the main contractor will be liable for at that date.
11. Cost accruals need to be reconciled on a regular basis to avoid the position where there is a large, accrued cost long after the works have been completed, thereby giving a false and pessimistic position.
12. Losses are recognized as soon as they are foreseeable, and profit is taken when it is earned and secure.

Limitations:

- The CVR technique might not lend itself to small and short-term projects or for small companies due to the time and resource requirement, which might be greater than the value derived from it.
- The production of the CVR relies on the skills and training of the personnel producing the CVR and bring inconsistency into the process. However, the use of templates and guidance can minimize this inconsistency but individual judgment and recollection of liabilities cannot be eliminated fully.
- Both cost and value must be taken at the same date, and if they fall on different dates, the data must be adjusted to match; otherwise, the method cannot produce accurate information.
- The reporting system and procedure can become too complex that, in many cases, it just ends up being a "box ticking" exercise with output that is not useful and the project team seeing it as requiring too much effort and a time-wasting exercise.
- The CVR technique can indicate that a project is running at a loss but what caused this loss will usually require further analysis and context.

S-Curve

The S-curve is a mathematical graph that depicts relevant cumulative data for a project such as cost or man-hours plotted against time. The S-curve graph shows the shapes of the project's budgeted cumulative spend and actual cumulative spend when plotted against time. It can then be used to show the difference between these cumulative spends by providing a side-by-side comparison. It derives its name from the shape of the graph for budgeted cumulative cost, which usually forms an "S" shape. The shape is caused by a natural progression of spending on most projects where the work of the project is usually slow at the start and takes some time to accelerate, increases sharply in the middle stage as progress is made, and slows down toward the end (see Figure 8.2). The point of maximum growth in the middle is called the point of inflection. During this period, lot of work

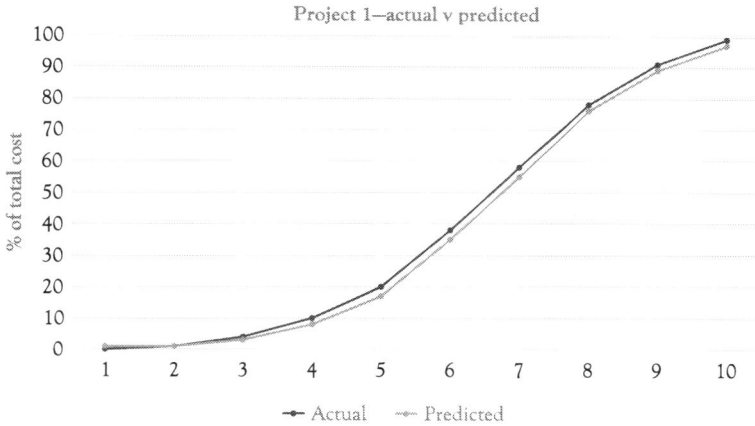

Figure 8.2 Typical S-curve

will be taking place to deliver the project and majority of the major costs are incurred. After the point of inflection, the growth begins to plateau, forming the upper part of the graph known as the upper asymptote where the project delivery pace stabilizes until it slows to completion. The S-curve usually provides a visual representation of whether the current spending on the project is under the budgeted amount or over budget as the project progresses by comparing the current S-curve with the baseline S-curve.

The form of the S-curve is determined by the start date, the end date, and the way the value of work done is assessed. Once a consistent approach has been established and the historical data analyzed, there are three significant variables that need analyzing: time, money, and the shape of the S (known as the route). Since the expectation is that the route is fixed, then only two variables are left (time and money). Further analysis can be carried out by comparing movement of the S-curve from period to period in order to obtain the current trend for the project so that remedial action can be implemented as necessary.

Benefits and Limitations of the S-Curve

Benefits of the S-Curve

- The main advantage of the S-curve is that when the actual cumulative project spending is plotted on the same graph, it can show easily whether spending is more than was budgeted or less.

- The S-curve graph shows what is happening on a project in relation to cost and spending visually and can be understood easily in order to act as necessary. The degree of alignment between the two graphs (current S-curve and baseline S-curve) will reveal the progress or lack of progress and if corrections need to be made to get back on track.
- As a tracking tool, it can be used for comparisons of different S-curves (such as cost S-curves, man-hours S-curve, target S-curve, and percentage complete S-curve) against the baseline S-curve to help in monitoring and controlling the project as required.

Limitations of the S-Curve

The S-curve doesn't show the causes of the differences between the planned and actual spend. For example, if the current cumulative actual cost is less that the planned cumulative cost, it might be due to either of the following:

- The work was completed on schedule or even ahead of schedule but at a lower cost than planned.
- The work was completed behind schedule but at a higher cost than anticipated.

The difference between these two is significant because the former means that future costs are likely to be less than budgeted, and the latter means that future costs look likely to exceed the budget. The best way of answering this question is through a method called earned value analysis (EVA), which is discussed in the next section.

Earned Value Analysis and Management

Earned value management (EVM) is a methodology used to measure and communicate the real physical progress of a project against the baseline and to integrate the three critical elements of project management (scope, time, and cost management). It considers the work completed, the time taken, and the costs incurred to complete the project and helps to evaluate and control project risk by measuring project progress in monetary terms (Vandervoorde and Vanhoucke 2005). The basic principle of EVM is that the value of a package of work or activity is equal to the amount of money budgeted for its completion. EVA (see Figure 8.3) is a technique of analyzing a project's progress at any given point in time, forecasting its completion date and final cost, and calculating variances in the schedule and budget as it progresses. The goal of the EVA is to support and facilitate the cost control process. The results of these analyses are used for EVM to manage identified variances, trends, and forecasts based on the EVA results.

EVA uses S-curves (see Figure 8.2), which examine the progress and forecast expenditure in terms of man-hours or money. The result is compared with the actual expenditure as the project progresses, or the value of the work done. In EVA, there are three major areas of control; these are commitments, value of work done, and expenditure. Therefore, S-curves can be produced for the value of work done, or commitment or even expenditure. The primary task of project control is to establish the exact position of the project from one time period to another in terms of the value of work done and compare this with the targets for each time period. Project control can comment on the validity of planning work by comparing planned and actual progress via the value of the work done.

EVA Measures

EVA uses three basic measures that are based on the actual costs incurred and cost estimate of a project. These are as follows:

- Planned value (PV) or budgeted cost of work scheduled (BCWS): This is the amount that is expected to be expended for the work scheduled at the present time.
- Earned value (EV) or budgeted cost of work performed (BCWP): This is the amount that is expected to be paid for the work that has been done at the present time.
- Actual cost (AC) or actual cost of work performed (ACWP): This is the actual cost of the work that has been completed at the present time.

The aforementioned three measures are then used to calculate a set of variances as detailed below:

- *The cost variance* (CV): This is the difference between the budgeted cost of work performed (BCWP) and the actual cost of work performed (ACWP), that is, CV = BCWP – ACWP.
- *The schedule variance* (SV): This is the difference between the budgeted cost of work performed and the budgeted cost of work scheduled (BCWS), that is, SV = BCWP – BCWS.

The project control status is based on the aggregate of the cost variance and schedule variance as explained above.

EVA is also used to give an indication of how far the project is ahead or behind schedule and how far the project is ahead or under budget by calculating a couple of indexes as explained below:

- Schedule performance index (SPI) is calculated as SPI = EV/PV. When the SPI is less than 1, greater than 1, or equal to 1, it indicates the project is ahead of schedule, behind schedule, or on schedule, respectively.
- Cost performance index (CPI) is calculated as CPI = EV/AC. When CPI is less than 1, greater than 1, or equal to 1, it indicates the project is under budget, over budget, or on budget, respectively.

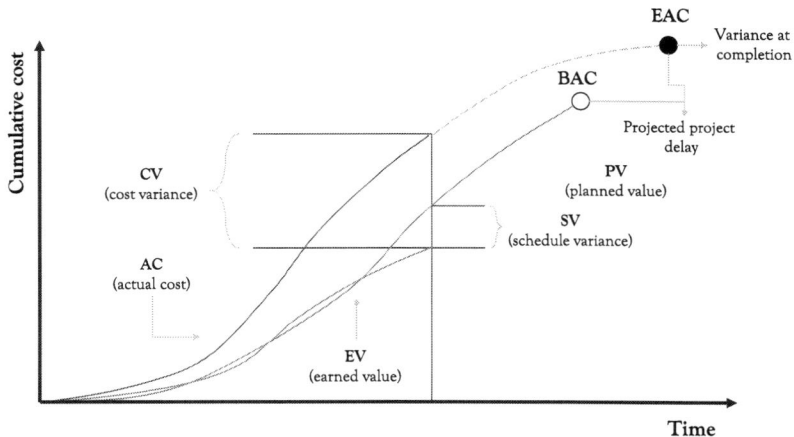

Figure 8.3 Typical earned value curve

EVA can also be used to forecast the performance of the project using the following indexes:

- Budget at completion (BAC): This is the total budget for all the works that need to be carried out on the project, it is calculated before the start or at the start of the project.
- Estimate at completion (EAC): This is used to give an indication of how much an activity of the project will cost at completion considering the rate achieved to date. This is calculated as follows EAC = Budgeted cost at completion/Cost performance index (CPI).
- Variance at completion (VAC): This is used to give an indication on how much over or under budget will the project be at completion considering the rate achieved to date. This is calculated as VAC = Budgeted cost at completion – EAC.
- Schedule at completion (SAC): This is used to give an indication of how long the activity or project will take to complete considering the rate achieved to date. It is calculated as SAC = Forecast duration/Schedule performance index (CPI).

In summary, the EVM is a system of approximation, the accuracy of which depends on the time and costs prepared in the estimate compared with the actual time and costs as work progresses. Therefore, the accuracy of the estimated and actual data is paramount to the successful application of EVM.

Advantages of EVA and EVM

- EVM is a comprehensive yet not oversophisticated methodology that allows the project team to measure and monitor the performance of a project. It brings together cost, time, and scope, which are three diverse but critical factors of a project to enable the analysis of the performance of a project as it progresses.
- It improves project performance, visibility, and accountability and provides data for proactive management action including

detailed project progress and forecast analysis data for effective decision making.

- EVA focuses on the measurement of cost and value. The variance analysis inherent in the EVA technique enables the assessment of the differences between the project baseline(s) and the actual performance.
- It can be used for forecasting on projects, which enables trend analysis and the ability to estimate the future performance of a project to identify the areas of improvement.
- The EVA measures can provide accurate results that can help identify discrepancies, change plans, correct mistakes, and make timely yet quality delivery possible.
- It helps achieve greater visibility and control of the project activities, which helps in responding to issues in a proactive manner giving the project a better chance of success.
- It provides a clear communication of the activities involved in delivery of a project and improves project visibility and accountability.

Disadvantages of EVA and EVM

- Earned value does not take quality of the work done into consideration because even though a project might be performing well on all the earned value metrics, but the quality of work may be below what is required.
- The cost of implementing EVM may sometimes discourage companies (especially small organizations) from using the method.
- Generally, computer software is required to use the technique, and the cooperation of different people and coordination among the different departments within the company are required to implement EVM.
- Similarly, it requires a significant amount of time to collect all the relevant data and information; for example, data in relation to actual costs needed to implement the method,

especially on big projects, while on small projects the effort required might be greater than the value derived from it.

- Since planned value is used as the baseline, it relies on prediction that brings uncertainty and subjectivity into the process. Therefore, even though a project might be performing well on all the EVA indexes, it might encounter delay in the future due to uncertainty involved in the planned value calculation.
- Once a project is over/under budget, CPI can remain the same for the remainder of the project, unless EV or AC changes significantly. The CPI is dependent on AC for accuracy. If AC does not include all appropriate costs, the CPI will not be accurate.
- The EVA is unable to distinguish between a critical task and a noncritical task. Therefore, even though the SPI may be indicating that the project is ahead of schedule, it might be because of many noncritical activities that are ahead of schedule eclipsing some critical activities that are behind schedule.

An Appraisal of the Suitability of the Cost Control Techniques

The previous sections have presented most of the classical project cost control techniques that can be used to control projects. Table 8.2 presents a summary of their applicability, strengths, and weaknesses.

From Table 8.2, it is evident that there is no flawless cost control technique, as each cost control technique has its own individual strengths and weaknesses, indicating that there is no one cap fits all cost control technique. For example, traditionally, cost control has been carried out using the S-curve technique showing the expected budget performance compared with the current performance S-curve, although the S-curve technique has some advantages such as that it can be drawn from experience of previous similar operations in the company at the estimating stage or it can be prepared on an arbitrary basis. The problem with the S-curve is that because the chart is frequently used as a means of control by plotting the actual expenditure curve against the budget curve, it is sometime wrongly assumed that whenever the actual expenditure curve

Table 8.2 Trait summary of existing project cost and time control techniques

Technique	Applicability	Strengths	Weaknesses
Profit or loss on each contract at valuation dates	Cost control	• Can be used to identify contract packages within the project that are currently experiencing over-spend and need attention to control cost • A straightforward and simple approach	• Doesn't provide a breakdown of the profit figure between types of work making up the section or contract of a project • Only shows which contract requires attention and does not specify between trades and activities • Offers a retrospective cost control approach
Unit costing	Cost control	• Quick and easy to implement • Helps understand the cost per unit as well as total cost	• Not a reliable method as it can produce large deviation from the accurate value
Standard costing	Cost control	• Provides a comprehensive cost control of the company from boardroom down to workforce • Helps to provide a close approximation of costs where actual costs for all activities in a company may be challenging to collect	• Not suitable for cost-plus contracts where actual costs are required • Not suitable in a fast-paced environment where costs change quickly • More suitable to a manufacturing environment
PERT/Cost	Scheduling and cost control	• Blends costs and work scheduled and allows cost and scheduling overruns to be identified and causes to be pinpointed quickly	• Cannot be applied easily directly to projects where the work is valued by a bill of quantities • Splintering up of large projects into smaller units may increase the overall problem of department coordination • Cost estimates in PERT/Cost may eventually end up as budgets and there is a tendency to inflate the budget in the initial planning stage

Cost value comparison	Cost control	• Can be used to compare project profitability and turnover against budget and forecast figure • Useful for monitoring project performance in terms of labor, plant, and material cost against original tender figures. • Useful as a monitor of the general performance when assessing tenders on other similar projects	• Both cost and value must be taken to a specific date because if they fall on different dates, then the method cannot be effectively used and a comparison cannot be drawn until one of the other is adjusted. • Reporting system and procedure can become overcomplex
S-curve	Cost control	• Useful in showing whether spending is more than was budgeted for or less when the actual cumulative project spending is plotted on the same graph • Can be drawn from experience of previous similar operations in the company	• Doesn't show the causes of the differences between the planned and actual spend
Earned value management	Cost control	• Integrates the three critical elements of project management (scope, time, and cost management) • Allows for three areas of control: commitments, value of work done, and expenditure	• A system of approximation, the accuracy of which depends on the time and cost prepared in the estimate compared with the actual time and costs as work progresses

keeps below the budget curve for value, the cost of the work is being controlled effectively and that the work is being carried out efficiently and profitably. However, from the control point of view, this combination of information is almost meaningless because the actual expenditure curve is not related to the physical quantity of the work, which has been carried out, nor the efficiency of operations. While the EVM, which is undoubtedly the best cost control technique in that it incorporates, time, cost, and scope, it also has some weaknesses such as its reliance on the estimate data and the perception that it is demanding of data. Therefore, it is important for project practitioners to understand the limitations of the cost control technique they are using and guard against them. This chapter has provided information that would help project practitioners in choosing the appropriate cost control technique for their project and using it in an informed way to enable effective cost control.

CHAPTER 9

Project Scope Management

Introduction

The scope of a project constitutes all the work to be carried out on the project for a given cost, to an agreed quality, and by a given time. Scope is one of the three elements of the "classic" iron triangle and triple constraints in project management. It is, therefore, an important aspect of project controls because without controlling the scope of a project, the project will experience scope creep. Scope creep occurs when a project's scope and deliverables change and expand in an uncontrollable way, beyond the scope that was originally planned, causing the project to experience cost overrun and time overrun. Scope creep can happen deliberately or additional elements of work may "creep" unintentionally onto the project as a result of various stakeholders on a project making changes to the project scope without considering its impact and project controls.

The importance of scope management is evident in the research that underpins the PCIM project control methodology where design and scope changes were found as the leading project control inhibitor for both cost and time control. Additionally, many other studies have shown the importance of scope control to project success; for example, the research by PMI (2020) found that scope creep affects 35 percent of projects. Successful project control is impacted by a clear definition of the scope of the project at the outset and the ability to manage change effectively through the project. These include scope management, such as controlling the quality of the contract documents, quality of response to perceived variations, and extent of changes to the contract. Little wonder why the PCIM research identified the effective management of scope and design changes as a leading factor influencing effective project cost and time control. The remaining sections of this chapter present an overview of some of the key principles of scope management.

Scope Management

The APM *Book of Knowledge* (BoK) (2019) states that scope management is the process whereby outputs, outcomes, and benefits of a project (see Chapter 11 for benefits management) are identified and controlled. In essence, scope management is the process required to ensure that the project includes all the work required to complete the project successfully. As summed up by the PMI (2021), scope management is primarily concerned with defining what is, or not, included in a project. Additionally, scope management helps in determining and documenting all the project goals, tasks, deliverables, deadlines, and budgets of a project right at the outset of the project, enabling the costing and scheduling of work and facilitating the management of changes and associated cost and time impact as the project progresses.

It is worthy of note that scope management is not about preventing changes from happening on a project since it is not always feasible to expect that a project will be completed without any change. The progressive elaboration characteristics of projects means that as the project progresses, more is known about the project and there might be a need to make changes to the original scope. Additionally, because projects are usually delivered over a time period and are not immediate deliverables like operations, the circumstances that the project was originally conceived might have altered (e.g., economic changes or client objectives) requiring changes to be made to the project.

Finally, scope management is aimed at managing changes in a controllable way with impact assessment carried out as well as the appropriate governance for approval in order to make the best decision for the project and its stakeholders. The aim of scope management is to prevent scope creep on a project, which can occur easily if a project scope is not properly defined, documented, and/or controlled. In addition to its control function, scope management also involves the process of quantifying what is included, and what is excluded to be delivered on a project and subdividing the scope of work into manageable work packages.

Components of Scope Management

Scope management involves three areas: initiation, scope planning, and scope control as shown in Figure 9.1.

Figure 9.1 Components of scope management

Initiation

The initiation component of scope management covers the rationale for the project and how it fits into the organization's strategy. Initiation is the first phase of a project's life cycle and is focused on starting up a new project. The project initiation phase of a project is where the business problem or opportunity that the project is required to solve or exploit, respectively, is identified. Additionally, the initiation phase of a project is where the business case (see chapter 11 for more on business case) for the project is developed. The business case presents the problems or opportunities for the project and the options available to solve the problems or exploit the opportunities and the preferred solution selected for implementation. In essence, the solution selected sets the context for the scope of work to be delivered because different options will have different scope. In addition to the business case, the initiation phase will usually be required to produce the following output in order to get the project established:

- *Project brief*: A statement of the situation, outlining the problem/opportunity.
- *Project proposal*: An outline either of a solution to the problem, or how to maximize the opportunity presented. This is issued in response to the brief.
- *Project charter*: Contains the project's terms of reference, that is, the formal approval of the existence of a project, including

assigning of project name and identification number (ID number). A project charter should be a tightly worded document outlining what is to be done and the project's boundaries. It formalizes the project and should be documented and approved by the relevant stakeholders in line with the governance arrangement of the project. The project charter should also include:

o The background to the project
o Key assumptions
o The business and other needs
o The scope of work
o Identification of key activities, budgets, and dates
o Comments on how the project is to be managed
o The role of the project manager (responsibility and authority) and reporting structure

Scope Planning

Project scope planning is concerned with the definition of all the work needed to meet the objectives of a project successfully. The aim of scope planning is to enable a clear identification of all the required work of a project, the documentation of the deliverables and outcomes, and the definition of the boundary conditions required to complete a project. Additionally, scope planning involves identifying the goals, objectives, tasks, resources, budget, and timeline of a project. Scope planning enables the project management team to have clear information about all the work that needs to happen on their project as well as the work that is not required. Furthermore, scope planning facilitates the updating and documentation of changes to the scope as the project progresses. In essence, it is the basis for control in a project.

At the heart of scope planning is scope definition. Scope definition is the identification, description, and documentation of all the work necessary to complete a project. A well-defined project scope is a necessity to ensure the success of a project. Project definition is achieved strategically through the project scope statement. The project scope statement establishes the project baseline and boundary conditions, which cannot be compromised without the approval of the project sponsor or responsible stakeholder as determined by the governance structure of an organization. Scope planning is implemented on a project through the work breakdown structure (WBS) (we look at this in detail later in this chapter) or product breakdown structure (PBS).

As contained in APM BoK (2019), a product breakdown structure (PBS) is a hierarchical structure of things that the project will make or outcomes that it will deliver; it decomposes a "main project's product" into its constituent parts in the form of a hierarchical structure. A project consists of deliverables; however, these deliverables are not what is referred to as products, it is the features of these deliverables that need to be specified by the users, and then need to be designed, developed, and tested, or reviewed, to ensure they meet the users' specifications that are products. In essence, the focus is on products to be produced, not the work to be done to produce them. Therefore, if the product is deemed to have met the specifications, then invariably the deliverable has been delivered correctly. For example, in a project, scheduling the project is an activity or project deliverable while the approved project schedule is a product. While in an IT project, an example of a project product is the user acceptance testing approval document. In contrast, the work breakdown structure (WBS) provides a hierarchical structure of project activities (see Section titled "The Work Breakdown Structure" later in this chapter and Figure 9.2), that is, the project "to-do list." The WBS focus is always on the work to be delivered and not the documents to confirm that the work has been carried out. For example, in a civil engineering project, "carry out compression testing" is part of the work while "approved compression testing certificate" is a product.

These breakdown structure tools (WBS/PBS) specify very clearly what is included, and just as importantly, what is excluded from the project (and is to be done "by others"). An important aspect of scope planning is decomposition of the work, that is, breaking the product and the work into tasks. Therefore, the use of breakdown systems depends upon the conceptual deconstruction of the project into its constituent products and parts. Breakdown structures systematically help with the planning for and communication of the work that needs to be done on a project. One of the key rules of breakdown structure is the popular "100 percent rule," which states that the WBS must include 100 percent of the work defined by the project scope and capture all deliverables (work to be completed, including project management activities).

Scope Control

All projects are subject to scope changes at some point during their life cycle. A scope change control system is a system that is designed to manage the change of scope process effectively. As mentioned earlier, only scope changes that are beneficial to the project should be allowed following a robust impact analysis. The project management team should install a robust system to monitor, evaluate, and approve all changes in accordance with the delegated authority governance structure of the project and organization before these changes are incorporated into the plan. Any scope change control process should be agreed upon by the project team and communicated to all the project stakeholders at the outset of the project as previously explained in Chapter 5. The process of scope control should be robust enough to cope with managing change to the deliverables of a project as they evolve through the project life cycle. The governance, administrative, and approval activities related to the identification, analysis, and communication of proposed changes should be made clear. There are two aspects to scope control. These are (1) scope development or design development and (2) scope changes or design changes.

Scope design and development: Design development is the process by which a specification, outline scope, schematic design, or high-level design and scope for a project is translated into the detailed design and scope that allows for the execution and delivery of the project.

Scope and design change: Scope and design changes involve variations to the project scope or design that have already been agreed. Any change to the scope or design of the project after the scope has been agreed upon will be a variation to the contractually agreed scope of the project. Therefore, it is important not to confuse design change (variations) with design development. In essence, in relation to the agreement and contractual sign-off of the project's scope, delivery timescale, and design before this milestone are "development. While changes to scope and design that happen once these have been contractually agreed upon or outside the parameter of the scope are design/scope changes, which are considered additional to the contract and may attract a time extension and additional costs since they are likely to impact the established contractual time and budget agreements.

Change impact analysis: It is important that any scope changes are assessed for impact by not just the scheduler (for time implication) and cost expert (for cost impact) but by the technical discipline responsible for the area of change. This will enable the project management team to understand the feasibility of implementing the change technically, the consequential effect on the technical aspect of the project as well as the resultant cost and time implications. Other areas of the project that need to be assessed for an impact of changes include procurement, production (resource impacts) quality, legal obligations (is the change permitted or will it infringe any legal obligations?), and risk (will the change introduce additional risks to the project that need to be mitigated or is the consequential risk significant enough to avoid the change?).

The Work Breakdown Structure

It is evident from this chapter that an important part of scope management and control is the work breakdown structure (WBS). Therefore, for completeness, this chapter concludes by looking at the concept of WBS in more detail. Projects can be broken down in a number of ways, for example, by functional areas, physical grouping, products (the PBS described earlier in the chapter), and activities of work (the WBS described earlier and discussed in detail here). The WBS is the most common way projects are broken down. The WBS, according to APM (2015), is used to break down a project into smaller elements and create packages of work to define responsibility for delivery and facilitate project control.

The WBS is vital for project control because cost and time control cannot be carried out effectively without the principle of the work breakdown structure. The WBS is the framework or skeleton upon which the whole project rests. It is the work scope organized into a detailed hierarchical format and ties all the three sides of the project iron triangle (work scope, schedule, and cost) together. As stated previously, the WBS is the breakdown of the project into all the activities and tasks needed to design, procure, implement, and complete the project. Furthermore, WBS helps present the physical subsystems to be developed and links the components of work to be done to each other and to the overarching project when finished. The relationship between WBS, cost, and time is that quite often the breakdown of cost is based on the WBS while the WBS informs the development of the schedule.

The WBS is the fundamental framework for defining the work content of the project, for organizing the cascade of activities, and for coding activities on a consistent basis. Typically, a work breakdown structure (see Figure 9.2) is organized into levels of detail as follows:

Level 0: The overarching project and the outcome or deliverable

Level 1: The overarching project schedule

Level 2: Work packages

Level 3: Group of activities or tasks that are required to deliver the work packages

Level 4: Individual activities or tasks

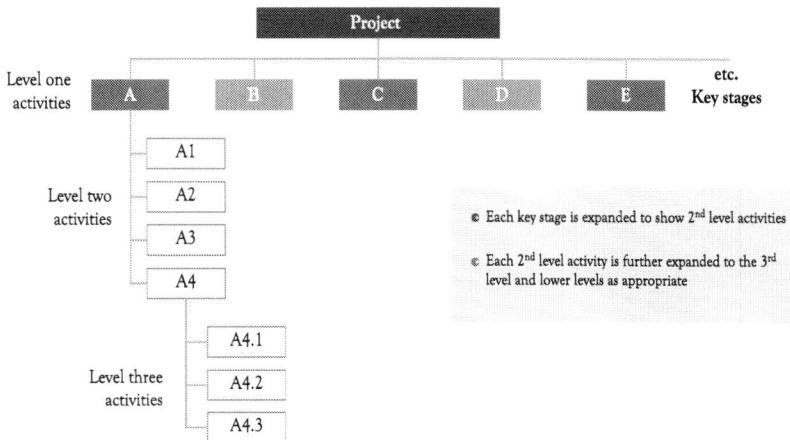

Figure 9.2 A typical work breakdown structure

The Purpose of Work Breakdown Structure in the Planning and Control Process

The WBS is crucial in achieving effective control of a project. As defined by the APM (2015), the WBS provides a common framework for the development of the planning and control of a project. Kezner (2017) goes further by asserting that the WBS is the single most important element of planning and control because it provides a common framework from which many of the activities of planning and control are implemented. For example, due to the WBS:

- The planning of a project can be carried out and documented more accurately, especially when a WBS code is assigned to all the work of the project;
- The overall project schedule can be simplified into smaller components and aggregated back to form the overall schedule in a logical manner enabling a better understanding of the project;
- Costs and budgets can be determined for the whole project and for various levels of the project;
- The key performance metrics of a project such as time, cost, and resources can be monitored;
- Reporting approach for the key performance metrics (including scope) of the project can be established to enable accurate reporting; and
- Ownership and responsibility for the completion of various areas of the project can be done easily and enables the production of a robust responsibility assignment matrix.

Conclusion

This chapter has shown the importance of scope management to the project control process. Scope control is the link between time control and cost control. This is because time control aims to control the planned scope of a project at the planned time while cost control aims to ensure that the cost of the scope of work being delivered is within the planned cost for that scope of work. A lack of control of the scope will invariably affect the cost and/or time of the project. Therefore, as far as projects are concerned, a clear change and scope control procedure should be installed that defines how changes are recorded, evaluated, authorized, and implemented in a controlled manner. The scope control process should define clearly the responsibilities, accountabilities, approval thresholds, and associated timeframes required to impact assess and approve a scope change request. Additionally, as part of the scope control process on projects, there should be a formal recording of change control requests and approvals. This should be undertaken using standardized templates or a software tool. The change control tracker should be up-to-date and include details about the scope change such as the change owner, the estimated cost, budget availability and associated timeframes, and impact on time, cost, quality, and project benefits.

The governance approach for accepting changes in projects should be structured and robust to achieve an effective project control. Therefore, the evaluation, approval, rejection, or deferment of scope change requests should be carried out in accordance with the agreed governance regime of an organization, for example, the delegated authority matrix. The practice in most projects is to send the design or scope change request to a change control board or panel for approval. As a minimum, the cost, schedule, technical, and quality impact should be assessed in a robust way and attached to change control requests. The change control board or panel should be made up of people with good authority in the business with the right balance of skills and experience. This will enable them to make the right decisions about the change request that do not threaten the ongoing viability of the project's business case, associated benefits, and is congruent with the project's objectives and the organization's strategy.

CHAPTER 10

Risk Management

Introduction

This chapter provides an overview of risk management, which was identified by the PCIM project control methodology research as the second most common factor that can inhibit effective cost and time control. Risk management is an inseparable and integral part of project management and critical for driving a project successfully. In fact, one of the benefits of applying project controls to a project is to unearth emerging risks to the cost and time performance of projects for corrective actions to be taken as appropriate. Risk management is also important for project control because during project delivery, risk analysis can be used to give probabilistic forecasts that provide levels of confidence in meeting the budget and schedule objectives using past project performance, which takes account of future risks and uncertainties in relation to the project.

Project Risks and Categorization of Risks

Risk is an uncertain event or set of circumstances that, should it occur, will influence the achievement of the project's objectives. It is the combination of the probability of an event and its consequence. Risks can be categorized according to their visibility or their origin.

Categorization of project risks based on their visibility

- *Known risks*: These are risks that are everyday feature of a situation.
- *Known unknowns*: These are risks that can be predicted or foreseen and anticipated.
- *Unknowns-unknowns*: These are risks that are due to events whose cause and effect cannot be predicted or emerge over time.

Categorization of project risks based on their origin

- *Global risks or external risks*: These are usually outside the control of the project parties and generally stem from the macroenvironment, for example, currency exchange, material cost inflation, economic downturn, health pandemic, and so on.
- *Elemental risks or internal risks*: These are risks associated with the key elements of a project; they are often specific to the project, for example, design failure, delay, scope creep, and so on.

Need for Systematic Approach to Risk Management

Risk management is the identification of future probable events, analysis of the events to determine probability of occurrence and their potential impact on project, and developing strategies for managing the risks. Effective risk management requires a systematic approach of (1) risk classification, (2) risk identification, (3) risk analysis, and (4) risk response. Figure 10.1 presents the systematic approach to risk management that should be adopted for projects.

Risk Classification

It is important to decide on a risk classification system appropriate for the project at the outset. This will be used to group the risks and help clarify the relationships among the risks. It helps kickstart the risk management process and bring some order into the mostly qualitative starting point. Different classification systems can be used, but mostly macrolevel classifications are employed. Some of the classification systems utilized are discussed below.

- *PEST or PESTLE*: This acronym stems from the classification of project risks in relation to their origin using the following macroenvironmental view: political risks, economic risks,

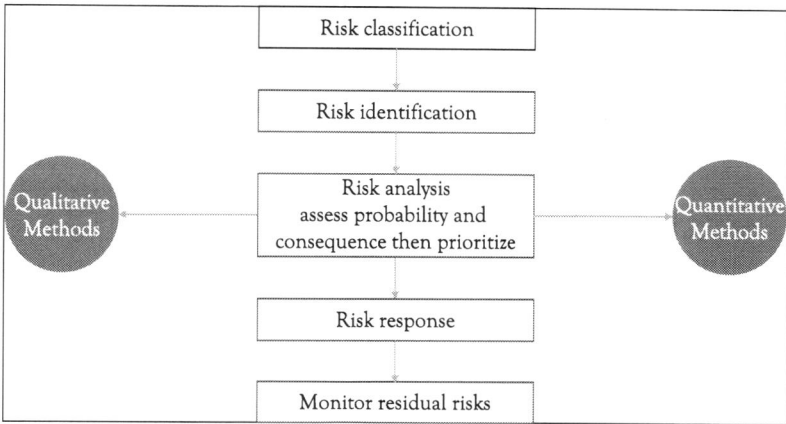

Figure 10.1 Systematic approach to risk management

social risks, technological risk, legal and contractual risks, and environmental issues that may affect the project.

- *SPORT*: This approach is similar to the PEST classification discussed previously and classifies risk according to macrolevel issues such as social risks, political risks, organizational risks, regulatory risks, and technological risks.

- *Disciplinary or organizational function approach*: This classification approach uses the discipline or organizational function that the risks relate to. This is the most common classification systems adopted for many projects. Examples of the classification includes health and safety risks, commercial risks, finance risks, information technology (IT) risks, and so on Figure 10.2 shows an example of this.

- *Predetermined approach by the organization*: Many organizations have devised their own risk classification system based on their management structure, functions, and culture. This would have usually emerged over time within the organizations and might have been devised by the finance department. The predetermined classification system may consist of one of the aforementioned approaches or a combination of at least two of them.

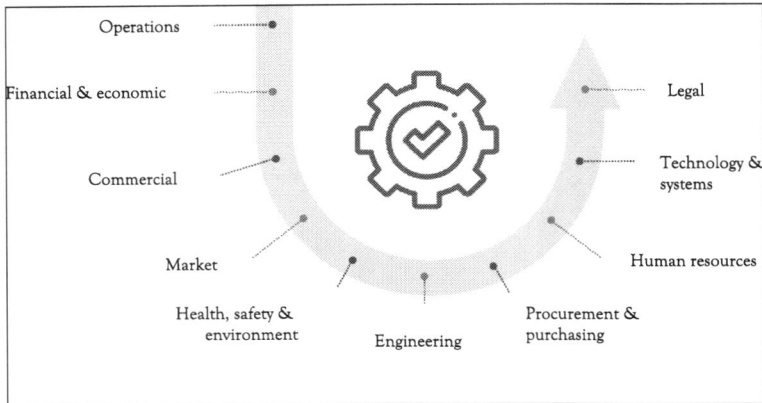

Figure 10.2 Disciplinary or organizational function project risk classification approach

Risk Identification

Risk identification is the process of unearthing and documenting the risks and threats to the successful delivery of a project in a comprehensive, practical, and structured manner. The aim of risk identification is to identify the maximum possible risks at the initial stage of a project. In essence, risk identification should involve the compilation of a list of risks that is comprehensive and as complete as possible. There are different methods, tools, and techniques that can be used, for example, documentation reviews, brainstorming, Delphi technique (see Chapter 6 for more information on the Delphi technique), interviewing, and so on. It is not usually possible to uncover the entire risks specific to the project at the initial stage because of the *progressive elaboration* characteristic of projects. The progressive elaboration concept of projects is that you know less about the project at the early stage such as the initiation and planning stages of a project compared to the later stages of the project when you have more information. In essence, you gain more information and knowledge about projects as you progress through a project's life cycle. There is no single best method for risk identification; however, a combination and usage of several risk identification tools can be effective.

Describing Risks Correctly

In practice, it is very common for risks to be described vaguely or incompletely, for example, *"specialist vending equipment may be delivered late."* This description is incomplete as it does not provide a good picture of the risk. Irrespective of the identification techniques used, it is essential to describe risks clearly based on the cause-and-effect relationship as depicted in Figure 10.3 and explained below.

- *Cause*: Description of the source of the risk, that is, the situation that gives rise to the risk. These are usually called risk drivers.
- *Risk*: Description of the area of uncertainty.
- *Effect*: Description of the impact(s) that the risk would have on the project objectives should the risk materialize.

Using the example provided above, the risk should be correctly described as below.

Correct description: Due to the Covid-19 pandemic in China (cause), there is a risk that the specialist venting system ordered from the country will now not be delivered on time (risk), which would delay the completion of the mechanical and electrical (M&E) work package (effect).

The Risk Register

The risks are recorded in a risk register maintained in a project. This could be on a spreadsheet or in a proprietary risk management software package.

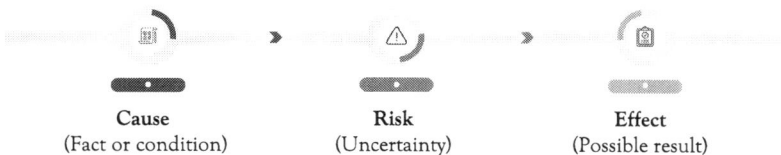

Cause	Risk	Effect
(Fact or condition)	(Uncertainty)	(Possible result)

Figure 10.3 How to correctly describe risks

The risk register provides a comprehensive description of the risks that may exist in the project. The risk register should provide the following information: risk identifier, description of the causes and the impact (cost and time), probability of impacts, timing of likely impacts, responses and mitigations plans, and effect, ownership of the management of the risk and so on. There are different ways of developing a risk register, but a consistent approach should be adopted during a project.

Risk Analysis

This is the process of digging deeper into the identified risks to understand them so that effective decisions can be made in relation to how they are managed. It is a prerequisite for effective risk management. Risk analysis can be carried out either qualitatively or quantitatively and this facilitates the ranking and prioritization of the identified risks, hence helping managers decide where actions are most needed (better allocation of resources). The assessment of risks, in general, can be categorized as qualitative risk analysis and quantitative risk analysis.

Qualitative Risk Analysis

This involves determining what impact the identified risks will have on the project objectives and the probability that they will occur. It also involves ranking the risks in priority order according to their effect on the project objectives. It helps determine if quantitative risk analysis should be performed or if it is possible to develop risk response plans straight away. The most common form of qualitative risk analysis is the probability/severity matrix also called a risk matrix. It is a qualitative method of analyzing risks that assesses and scores in simple numerical terms the likelihood that a risk event will occur, and the potential severity of the impact that the risk event will have. The qualitative assessment provides a rating scale by significant levels, for example, "high," "moderate," and "low" of the consequences and the probability of risks. This is usually depicted visually using a matrix as shown in Figure 10.4.

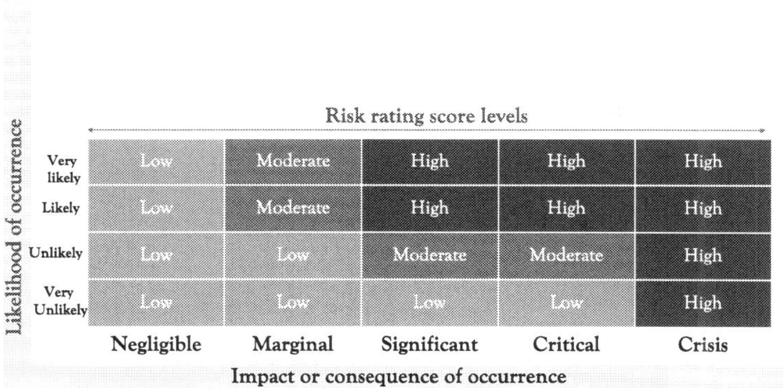

Figure 10.4 *Qualitative risk analysis: Impact and likelihood*

Quantitative Risk Analysis Techniques

This is a more rigorous risk analysis process and involves a numerical analysis of the overall effect of risks on the project objectives such as cost and schedule objectives. It is focused on assigning quantifiable quantities to the identified risks of a project and carrying out robust numeric analysis to examine the viability of a project's cost or time objectives because of risks posed to them. It enables a more detailed understanding of (1) the probability of meeting the project's objective, given all known risks, (2) how much the overrun or delay to a project could be, and therefore how much contingency is required to achieve the company's desired level of cost and time certainty, and (3) the areas of the project that pose the most risk because of the project's profile and financial quantum of all the identified risks on a project. Quantitative risk analysis provides a more detailed understanding of the risks facing a project including various probability levels and helps to decide on the contingency sum required for the project. There are several quantitative risk analysis techniques that can be utilized for projects. These are described below.

Sensitivity Analysis

Sensitivity analysis is a form of risk analysis that can help determine the effect of a risk on the whole project when a risk variable changes. It is a practical method of investigating risks on a project by varying the values of key factors and measuring the outcome, thereby highlighting the key factors that may affect the project outturn, should they be varied. Due to this, the sensitivity analysis is on occasion called a "what-if" analysis. It highlights the key factors that could have a significant impact on the overall project should they change. In practice, a sensitivity analysis should be performed for all identified risks to establish which have potentially the highest impact on the project outcome.

Decision Tree

Decision trees are a pictorial method of showing a sequence of interrelated decisions highlighting possible courses of action and future possible outcomes (see Figure 10.5). It is a quantitative method of modeling options for delivering an investment project that shows the possible effects of each project decision given the prevailing risks associated with the outcome of each option. The aim of the decision tree is to produce an expected value (EV) for each option in the decision-making process.

The EV is calculated as follows:

• Draw a decision tree with the possible options and their consequences. Start drawing using nodes and branches with nodes representing an option and branches representing alternative outcomes.

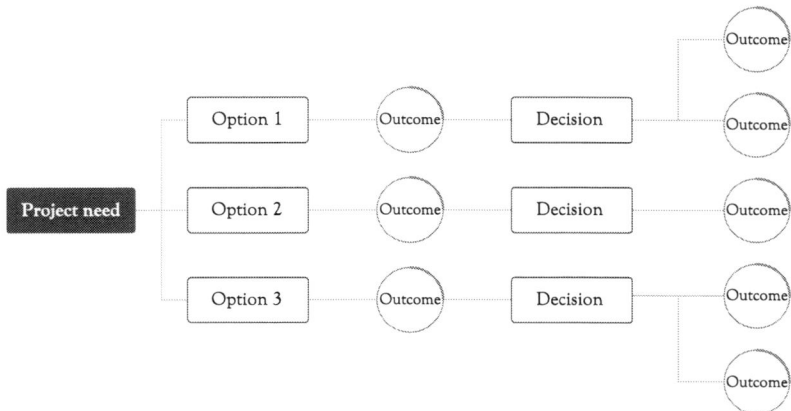

Figure 10.5 Decision tree

- Assign each outcome a probability of occurrence allowing for all the outcomes of the options in contention for delivering the investment project to be explored to support the best course of action.
- Determine the risks and allocate payoffs for each possible outcome.
- Calculate the expected monetary value for every chance node by multiplying the allocated payoff with the assigned probability in order to determine which options(s) is expected to provide the most value.

Costing Risk: Expected Monetary Value

Risks usually impact a project and this impact usually has a cost implication. In order to plan for the impact of risks and set a realistic budget to deliver a project, it is important to cost risks. Costing of risk is the most basic quantitative method for calculating a risk allowance in a project. The process of costing risk is like the process of calculating the expected value in the decision tree quantitative risk analysis approach. There are two approaches: the simple costing method and the three-point estimating or probabilistic method.

Simple Costing Method

- Assign a likely cost to all the risks in the risk register along with a, usually subjective, probability of occurrence. Then multiply the cost by the probability to give an expected value as shown in Table 10.1.
- Total the expected value for each risk to get an overall risk allowance.
- Expected value = probability × cost impact.
- For example, the delay to completion risk has a 15 percent chance of occurring and may cost £400,000.
- Therefore, the expected value of the risk is 0.15 × £400,000 = £60,000.

Table 10.1 Example of expected monetary value

Risk	Cost impact	Probability (%)	EMV
Delay to completion	£400,000	15	£60,000
Procurement of inexperienced contractor	£200,000	10	£20,000
Productivity	£180,000	15	£27,000
Estimating inaccuracy	£250,000	10	£25,000
Contractor bankruptcy	£500,000	4	£20,000
Poor quality	£300,000	5	£15,000
Overall risk allowance			**£167,000**

Three-Point Estimating or Probabilistic Method. The probabilistic method is a more in-depth version of the simple method and sometimes called "three-point estimating," which is carried out as follows.

Apply a meaningful, probability to each risk in the register over a range of three assumptions (best, likely, and worst case). The probabilities for all three should equal to 1 (100 percent).

Use these to generate an expected value per assumption by multiplying the probability of each assumption by the financial impact of each assumption. Then add the three assumptions to generate an expected value for each risk.

Total all the expected value for all the identified risks to get an overall risk allowance from the risk register.

Monte Carlo Simulation

Monte Carlo simulation is another probability-based method of risk analysis. It is a computerized mathematical technique that defines the consequences of each risk by a probability distribution. The simulation creates multiple scenarios by randomly sampling values from the probability distribution with modern computers allowing hundreds of trials.

Quantitative Schedule Risk Analysis (QSRA)

The QSRA uses statistical techniques to test the level of confidence in achieving the project completion date. This involves the application of Monte Carlo simulation to the schedule of a project for the risk information of project activities to be linked to the baseline schedule. The two elements of the QSRA are duration uncertainty, which provides a minimum, most likely, and maximum spread of activity durations, and risk impact, which assesses the minimum, most likely, and maximum impacts. This enables sensitivity information of each of the activities on the project schedule to be analyzed in relation to the possible effect of the uncertainty stemming from them on the eventual project duration.

Quantitative Cost Risk Analysis (QCRA)

QCRA is used to analyze the cost certainty of a project to estimate the probable cost outturn. This involves the application of Monte Carlo simulation to the risk register to enable the computation of the cost of the risks facing a project. This facilitates the identification of current impact of the risks to the project budget and informs what contingency should be provided. The overarching aim of the QCRA on a project is to estimate the right level of financial contingency to add to the project estimate to account for the identified risks on the project. Therefore, to implement a QCRA on a project, the risk register needs to be costed fully with the likely impact of a risk identified as a three-point estimate similar to the PERT/cost described in Chapter 8, that is minimum, most likely, and maximum. A QCRA is performed using risk software packages (such as @Risk, Active Risk Manager, Primavera Risk Analysis) where cumulative distribution graphs such as the S-curves can be created to inform outcomes at various confidence intervals between 0 and 100 percent.

Risk Response

The risk response stage during risk management comprises the utilization of an appropriate mitigation strategy (a future plan of action involving considered and agreed methods of dealing with every identified risk). The main aim of any response and mitigation strategy is to initiate and implement appropriate action to prevent the risks from occurring. All strategies must be agreed, recorded, and documented with responsibilities clearly stated and communicated to the appropriate stakeholders. Risk response can be passive or active.

- *Passive risk response*: This implies the rejection of a considered mitigation strategy; at its best, it serves merely to monitor identified risks. This is not usually recommended in a project.
- *Active risk response*: This implies the formulation of a mitigation strategy that may be one, or a combination, of the following risk mitigation strategy discussed below.

Avoidance Risk Response Strategy

This may involve changing some aspect of the project to prevent the threat from happening or not have an impact. Aspects of the project that may be changed include the scope, procurement route, activity sequence, design type, and so on.

- *Example*: On an IT project that has a tight delivery timescale, deciding against procuring a payroll IT system that is renowned for its difficulty to be integrated with other financial systems to another payroll IT solution that is more expensive but easy to integrate with other financial systems.

Reduction Risk Response Strategy

This is usually a proactive action by any of the project partners to either reduce the probability of the threat from occurring through some form of control and/or reduce the impact of the threat if it occurs at all.

- *Example*: To reduce the likelihood of an imported equipment to be fitted in a hospital project being delayed at a country's port with a two-week turnaround for clearing of such equipment, it is ordered to arrive eight weeks before being fitted. To reduce the impact should this risk occur, the activity is planned to ensure it doesn't fall on the critical path.

Fallback Risk Response Strategy

This involves putting in place a contingency for the actions that will be taken to reduce the impact of the threat should the risk come to fruition. It is a reactive measure and only affects impact but has no bearing on the probability of the risk.

- *Example:*
  To reduce the risk of an American construction company misunderstanding the contract documents in German during a negotiation process for a project in Germany, a specialist legal documents translator from the host country was arranged to meet the team at the airport and join the negotiating party, but as a fallback John Smith who has a degree in German is also included as part of the team.

Transfer Risk Response Strategy

This is when a third party takes on the responsibility for some of the financial impact of the risk. It is a form of risk reduction but with only the mechanism to reduce the financial impact of the risk.

Example:

- Taking insurance for the risk of vandalization of an ongoing gas power generating project in a city with a reputation for environmental protests and activism.
- Liquidated damage clause (this is a contract provision that specifies an amount to be paid to the owner of the project by the party executing a project if the project is not completed on time, for example, £10,000 weekly until completion) in a project contract for a delay to completion of the project by the contractor delivering a software implementation project.

Acceptance Risk Response Strategy

This is a conscious and deliberate decision to retain a threat because it is deemed more economical to accept it than try to mitigate it. This approach is ideal for those risks that will not create a high amount of loss if they occur and the severity of the risk is lower than the risk tolerance level.

- Risk Tolerance: Risk tolerance is the level of risk above the risk appetite that an organization or a project is willing to accept.
- Risk Appetite: Risk appetite is the level of risk an organization or project has decided to accept to achieve its objectives. Risk appetite comprises two dimensions first, the attitude of an organization toward risk and second, risk capacity, that is, how much risk an organization or project can bear.

Example:

- There is a 5 percent chance that an imported specialist system will not be compatible with the electrical system of a metro rail project when installed in the country it is imported to. To mitigate this, a local engineer will have to make it compatible, causing a one day delay to the activity that has a float of two weeks anyway.
- Hence it is probably not worth the effort/money to act on this but rather wait and see if the equipment will not be compatible and then call the engineer.

Sharing Risk Response Strategy

This is a risk response mechanism where the key partners to a project portion a risk. This is usually done through a pain-gain formula. This is where both parties share the gain from the risk not occurring and share the pain if the risk does come to fruition.

- *Example:*
  Stipulating a pain-gain agreement in the contract of a highly complex nuclear power project that if the project is delivered within budget, 25 percent of the £370 million contingency will be shared equally between the contractor and the client. But if delivered above the budget, the additional cost will be borne equally by the contractor and the client.

The significance of a risk in relation to a project will determine the project team's response, see Table 10.2 for risk response strategy good practice. Good practice demands that all risks, irrespective of their significance should have a mitigation strategy. However, from the author's experience, the reality is that the project management team will use the analysis stage to prioritize the risks as depicted in Figure 10.1 earlier. Therefore, low level risks may be accepted by the project team if their impact is deemed insignificant to the project. However, for moderate level risks, the recommended good practice is to always apply mitigation measures that will help reduce or remove the risks from the project or/and develop mitigating measures to reduce the impact of each risk. High level risks are usually seen as a significant threat to the project with the recommended good practice response to deal with these high level risks is for the project management team being proactive in dealing with these risks. This proactive response for high level risks could be elimination of the risk, transferring the risk to a party best able to manage the high risk or avoidance. In some cases, in the absence of an effective response to a high level risk, the avoidance response strategy may mean the termination of a project.

Table 10.2 Risk response strategy good practice

Level of risk	Recommended response strategy
• Low level risk	• May be accepted if the impact on the project is insignificant or impact recoverable easily • These types of risks need to be monitored for any increase in their impact and mitigating measures need to be developed if impact becomes higher than acceptable
• Moderate level risk	• Need mitigating measures to be applied to eliminate or reduce the likelihood of the risk • Effective control measures need to be established to limit and mitigate impact • The effectiveness of the mitigation and control measures need to be monitored and improved as required
• High level risk	• Eliminate or avoid if possible • If elimination or avoidance is not possible, requires a proactive, robust, and effective response • Monitor and review response to the risk proactively to ascertain continued effectiveness or whether elimination of the risk is now possible • May require transfer to another party • May require termination of the project in the absence of an effective or a viable risk response

Overview of Supplier Performance Management, Business Case, and Benefits Management Processes

Introduction

This section provides an overview of key supporting project management processes to cost, scope, and time control, for example, supplier performance management, which was identified by the PCIM methodology research as one of the top five factors that can inhibit effective cost and time control. The chapter also provides an overview of the business case process since the performance requirements for projects from an organizational perspective including cost, time, and technical requirement/scope are set out in the business case. An overview of benefits management is also provided as this is what project controls seeks to protect through effective control. A project that has not been controlled effectively will have its benefits eroded, therefore, project control interacts with the benefit management process.

Overview of Supplier Performance Management

Supplier performance in organizations is part of supply chain management, which is the set of processes and steps that an organization uses to acquire the various resources needed to create its products or projects (e.g., IT systems, buildings, roads, dams, etc.) and services (project management advice, architectural design services, statutory audit, marketing consultancy, etc.). Supplier performance is the flow of the entire set of activities involving the administration and flow of resources required to produce and deliver an organization's product or project, which is, therefore, important. Consequently, contractors, suppliers, and subcontractors are important for effective project control in organizations involved in projects. This is because many projects and project services are delivered with the help of third parties either delivering an aspect of the project or supplying important materials, technology kit, software system, specialist consultancy service, and so on required for the project. The generic term in business for these categories of third parties is suppliers. These suppliers could be contractors, their subcontractors, professional service advisers, and suppliers of equipment, materials, plant, and so on required for a project. Additionally, the research underpinning the PCIM project control methodology identified nonperformance of subcontractors and suppliers as one of the top five inhibitors to project cost and time control. Therefore, even though this book is not a procurement management or supply management book, for completeness, it is considered important to briefly discuss supplier performance management.

What Is Supplier Performance Management?

Supplier performance management involves the measurement, analysis, and management of the performance of suppliers in an organization. Supplier performance management allows an organization to realize the best value from their suppliers by minimizing costs, managing risks, and driving continuous improvement. Supplier performance management consists of the following activities: developing performance indicators, evaluation of suppliers, data collection, performance analysis, and performance review and feedback.

Developing Performance Indicators

As part of supplier performance, it is important to identify the performance indicators (PIs) and key performance indicators (KPIs) that suppliers need to be evaluated against. In selecting these KPIs, it is important to align the PIs and KPIs with organizational goals and objectives. This is because a lack of alignment of the supplier performance measures with organizational objectives can lead to an incongruence in performance measures of the contractor, subcontractor, or that of the supplier, which may have an impact on cost, quality, and delivery. Additionally, KPIs need to be active; it is not sufficient to just rely on lagging indicators as they only measure historic performance. Active KPIs comprise of leading indicators that can predict outcomes process as well as directional indicators that can be used to measure trends in the delivery of a service so that remedial action can be taken proactively. Table 11.1 shows an example of a KPI table for the suppliers delivering projects for a company.

Evaluation Approach

One of the most important aspects of supplier performance measurement is the design and implementation of an evaluation approach suitable for the organization. It is useful to utilize both quantitative and qualitative evaluation for supplier evaluation. Quantitative evaluation involves computing the actual performance of suppliers in relation to agreed

Table 11.1 Example of a supplier performance indicator

KPI	Rationale	Measure	Weight of ranking
% Bids of opportunity	Measurement of the suppliers' interest in bidding for projects	=(Number of bids made within a period)/(Number of opportunities within the period) × 100	10%
% Share of projects	Measurement of the suppliers' contribution to supporting the company in delivering their planned projects	=[(Number of projects to contract within a period)/(Number of projects to contract within the period] × 100	15%
Satisfaction: Service	Measurement of the level of satisfaction of service that is being provided by the suppliers	(Summation of all scores within a period)/(Number of scores within the period)	30%
Quality of the project delivered	Measurement of the level of satisfaction in relation to the project meeting the quality specified	(Summation of all scores within a period)/(Number of scores within the period)	30%
Satisfaction: Defects	Measurement of the level of satisfaction of impact of defects at handover	(Summation of all scores within a period)/(Number of scores within the period)	15%

quantitative metrics to measure the performance of the supplier in relation to objectives that are important to the delivery of the service such as delivery quality, responsiveness, financial health, value for money, cost reduction, innovation collaboration, ESG (environment, social, and governance), and so on. The most effective supplier performance measurement approaches are those that do not only rely on quantitative performance data but also utilize qualitative information to provide depth, richness, and context to the quantitative supplier performance data. The qualitative supplier performance data will cover metrics like engagement, culture and value alignment, opinions on satisfaction, self-reflection, improvement ideas, bottlenecks, and so on.

Information Collection

Data and information about performance should be collected regularly at periodic intervals from suppliers. A successful supplier performance management process will rely on good quality data and information. Once the evaluation approach has been designed, the available information collection method required to gather data from suppliers should be assessed and reviewed. If there is no information collection method available or if not suitable, effort should be made to develop an appropriate supplier performance data collection process and associated instruments such as supplier questionnaire and satisfaction survey. In designing the supplier data collection process and system, it is important to consider tools like questionnaires (web-based or paper), focus groups, system reports, face-to-face or virtual meetings, site visits, and so on. It is always useful to develop supplier performance KPI handbook that will explain the KPIs and how they will be collated and collected to make it clear to suppliers as well as staff operating the process.

Performance Data Analysis

Once there is a mechanism in place to collect performance data from suppliers periodically, the next step is to review and analyze the supplier performance data collected. To analyze the data efficiently, effort should be geared at collecting data that can be analyzed to enable a comparison of suppliers' performance. One of the ways of doing this is to collect quantitative data and use performance score cards across predetermined themes. The analysis should be objective and include the same category of information for similar suppliers or supplies delivering the same service. It is also important to plan the collection of data from suppliers to cover the same period to enable consistency of analysis. However, this might not be possible as not all suppliers might be delivering to the organization at the same period and so performance data might be collected at different periods and economic contexts. Therefore, it is important that the review and analysis of data cover the key factors that might make the analysis and comparison of contractors not equivalent. The use of software tools for the analysis should help deal with this challenge and aid with normalizing performance data across suppliers over different periods.

Monitoring supplier performance proactively can ensure that exceptions to policies are tracked and personnel and resources are assigned to address the problem quickly. Alerts and notifications can provide up-to-the-minute information to company personnel, letting them know of changes in supplier performance. Having a computer system that can take the analyzed data and present it in a report or visual format will improve accessibility for relevant stakeholders and enable quick and easy review of the information.

Reporting

The supplier performance process is not complete without reporting. The reporting aspect of this process includes reporting of performance internally within the organization as well as reporting and engagement with the suppliers themselves. For the process to be efficient and consistent, it is advisable to design a report that can present the information from suppliers in a way that provides insight in a quantitative way as well as in a qualitative context. The report should be assured for accuracy and quality internally within the organization. The supplier performance report will provide an insight on suppliers' performance against the agreed PIs and KPIs. Therefore, the performance baseline against which improvements can be measured will need to be defined. The report should be used to facilitate supplier relationship management discussions with the relevant suppliers to enable continuous improvement and addressing of emerging problems. Additionally, the tool that will be used to measure supplier performance should be accompanied by the performance indicator schedule and the scoring methodology so that it can be understood by the supplier and the client staff using the tool. The KPIs should be based on benchmarks from industrywide best practices. Finally, best practice requires that performance data should be collected from more than one perspective to provide a more rounded insight into the performance of the suppliers. Therefore, techniques such as a 360-degree client–supplier satisfaction feedback survey are now collected periodically, analyzed, and reported.

Review and Feedback

As part of the supplier performance management of an organization, it is important to seek active feedback on the operation of the supplier management process from the participants in the process including the suppliers being monitored. The feedback on the supplier performance measurement process, its effectiveness in relation to the provision of insights on the performance of suppliers, and enhancement of positive behaviors among suppliers should be used to improve the supplier performance management process and the experience of all stakeholders involved in it continually (see Table 11.2 for good practices in supplier performance management).

Table 11.2 Good practices in the supplier performance management process from a real-life organization

Background
The author has had the experience of reviewing the supplier performance management process of organizations. A summary of good practices found in some of the organizations the author had consulted with is provided below.
Strategy and vision
• First, there is a need to have a vision document and policy in place to provide direction, consistency, and clear message in relation to supplier performance management within the organization. This strategy was in place in organizations with leading supplier performance management practice and had been endorsed by senior management.
• In support of the supplier performance policy and vision document, a supplier performance management plan had also been developed to guide the implementation of the supplier performance requirements. The plan was developed in detail and provided the necessary direction concerning the implementation of supplier performance management in the organization with roles, responsibilities, accountabilities, timeframe, and effective use of resources.

Table 11.2 (Continued)

Implementation

- A detailed performance indicators schedule was also in place, which was used to monitor the performance of contractors and suppliers. The process for evaluating the performance of the suppliers was documented and explained in detail with the suppliers aware of the process and scoring methodology.
- Supplier performance management was also being carried out within the structure of formal policy, procedure, and vision, which enabled consistency of the supplier performance management process.

Governance

- The team delivering the supplier performance management process was accountable to senior management through a formal organizational structure.
- Senior management had a process for gaining assurance on the implementation of supplier performance process through periodic progress updates and reporting. There was a formal schedule of regular meetings, updates, and reporting regime.

Management information and risk management

- Some organizations had developed a contractor and supplier risk dashboard to consolidate management information. The financial dashboard for key suppliers included share price tracking for the last year as well as for recent previous years (for example, the last three years). The risk dashboard also contained the risk profile of suppliers and contractors, which tracks a supplier or contractor's share shorting over time as well as the H-score and risk indicator trend over time. The H-score is used to predict a company's likelihood of bankruptcy by analyzing a company's financial health using published financial results such as profitability, liquidity, working capital management, debt, and equity.
- The financial dashboard was being monitored by the procurement department with senior management also having access to the supplier risk dashboard.
- There was a supplier management risk framework, which used the dashboard system to trigger alerts if the supplier financial metrics dropped below the required level.
- Regular customer service survey and information on contractors' performance against the KPIs were obtained and the performance baseline against which improvements can be measured was defined.
- Financial information on supplier organizations from several sources was collated and the information used to track the financial metrics of the supplier organization, which was visible to the senior leadership team and was discussed during management meetings.
- The supplier organizations' financial metrics were also monitored by the commercial management information team to be aware when the financial metrics fall below a certain threshold so that risk management action can be taken.
- Supplier failure contingency plans were developed for key suppliers that were deemed to be at the risk of encountering financial challenge or collapse.

Overview of the Business Case Process for Projects

This book will be incomplete without providing an overview of the business case process because it is the business case that sets out the justification for the project and what success in relation to the project looks like from a financial, economic, and operational perspective in an organizational view, in essence cost, time, scope, and technical requirement/specification from a project dimension. The project business case is required to enable projects to deliver their intended output and benefits as it facilitates the proper scoping, planning, and cost justification of the project from the outset. The process of developing the business case involves determining the strategic context and carrying out a strategic assessment, making a case for the project and exploring the preferred way forward, that is, the business justification for the project. It also includes determination of the value for money, ascertaining affordability, and funding requirements.

The business case for a project should describe the reasons for the project, the scope of the change from the project, the justification for undertaking the project, the estimated cost of the project, the risks associated with the project, and the expected business benefits and savings. A well-developed business case will enable an organization to understand, influence, and shape the project's success early in the project's life cycle (see Table 11.3 for business case good practices). The business case also provides the basis for the project's postinvestment review plan to verify that the assessment of whether the outcome was successful. A project business case usually contains the following:

- *Reason for the project*: This should explain the reasons why the project is required in the business options. The various options that have been considered to deliver the required need of the organization should be described with the chosen option indicated, as well as the justifications for its selection.
- *Benefits expected*: Details of the benefits that would be derived from implementing the project should be included. The benefits should be defined in quantifiable terms. Benefits may also be assessed in negative terms such as what will happen if the project is not implemented. See the section titled "Overview

of the Benefits Management for Projects" later in this chapter for more details.

- *Risks*: The key risks facing the project should also be assessed as part of the business case; this is important so that projects outside the risk appetite of the business are not taken forward.
- *Cost estimate*: The estimated cost for delivering the project should be included in the business case. The approach for estimating the cost of the project should be robust and free from optimism bias.
- *Timescales*: The time for delivery for the project should also be indicated, and a summary of the current project plan and the time estimate should be included.

Table 11.3 Business case good practices

1. The project business case should be prepared following the approval by senior management of the mandate and project brief.
2. The business case needs to be backed up with evidence and the assumptions that the business case is based on need to be transparent and available for review.
3. Consideration also needs to be given to the constituents of the investment committee who will make the decision to proceed to ensure that the right people are included.
4. Importance needs to be placed on the committee having the right information to make the business case decision and the assurance process for the information.
5. The ownership of the business case will be the executive requesting the project such as the business unit head. The executive will also be responsible for ensuring that the project objectives, cost, and benefits are correctly aligned with the business strategy.
6. The executive should facilitate the development of the business case by delegating to an appropriate person such as a project manager but the data and information for its development will be provided by the business and the responsibility for the development of an accurate and effective business case sits with the executive.
7. Information from the project brief should be used to develop the business case.
8. Formal approval of the business case is required from the executive to ensure that senior management is committed to the project.
9. During each stage of the project, the business case should be reviewed to confirm that the project remains on track and to check that the business case remains valid within the business context.
10. At project closure, the business case should be used to confirm that the project has delivered the required outcome and that the benefits from the project can be realized as planned.
11. The business case should not just be used as an approval document; it should be a working document and the basis for strategic management, monitoring, and evaluation during and after project delivery (including benefit realization) of the project.

- *Sensitivity analysis*: Sensitivity analysis also needs to be performed during the evaluation of the business case to test the boundaries of the project by varying the values of key factors and measuring the outcome, highlighting those that may have a high impact on the project outturn when they change (see chapter 10 for more on sensitivity analysis).
- *Investment appraisal*: The investment appraisal of the project compared to the investment approval criteria of the company with the do-nothing option as a baseline should also be undertaken and included in the business case. There is a standard financial/economic model that is used in evaluating business cases and this covers the five-case model by considering the following five dimensions:
  o Strategic
  o Economic
  o Commercial
  o Financial
  o Management

Overview of the Benefits Management for Projects

Projects are driven by the need to deliver benefits on their own or as part of a program. A benefit is the measurable improvement resulting from an outcome of a project, which contributes toward one or more organizational objectives. The projects and associated program, when completed, will deliver outputs, which will create new capability(ies) for an organization. These capabilities are then transitioned into outcomes, which enable the realization of benefits. These benefits then contribute to the actualization of an organization's corporate objectives. The management of benefits is usually carried out as a four-step cycle of benefits identification, benefits realization planning, benefits delivery (tracking and realization), and benefits review. These are discussed below.

Benefits Identification

The benefit management process commences during the business case stage of the project (see the section titled "Overview of the Business Case

Process for Projects" earlier in this chapter" for more details) by identifying the likely benefits that will result from the delivery of the project. These benefits should relate back to an organization's corporate objective. Identification of the benefits should be carried out by engaging the key stakeholders to generate the initial list of benefits. Benefits could then be categorized as:

- Value (economic benefits, effectiveness benefits, efficiency benefits)
- Financial impact (cashable, noncashable)
- Corporate objectives they support
- Stakeholder management
- Timeline
- Level of risk

As part of the benefits identification process, how the project will lead to a benefit from the project output and capabilities it provides to an organization also needs to be mapped. The benefits map will show the relationship between the project output, capabilities, outcomes, benefits, and the corporate objectives. Additionally, as part of the benefit identification process, benefit profiles should be developed as a minimum for each of the key benefits identified. The benefit profile describes a single benefit with its attributes and interdependencies. The benefit profile for each benefit will also include the description of the benefit and an operational owner.

Benefits Realization Planning

Once the benefits have been identified, the organization will need to plan for the delivery of these benefits by allocating them to an owner who will be responsible for their delivery. The area of the business affected by the benefit should be responsible for its delivery. A benefit realization plan should then be developed, which will provide a complete view of all the benefits, their dependencies, and the forecast timescale for realization. The benefit realization plan should be developed during the investment phase of the project as part of the investment project plan and revised as more information emerges. The benefit realization plan will be used to track the realization of benefits in relation to the project once the project is completed and in the operational phase such as the development of a new IT system in an organization, with speed of operation and efficiencies expected as a key benefits of the completed IT system project.

Benefits Delivery and Realization

This is when the capabilities delivered by the projects are converted into outcomes and deliver new or improved operations through speed, efficiencies, accuracy, improved quality, and so on. During benefit realization, it is important to measure the benefits. Therefore the metrics that will be used to track progress toward realizing the benefit will need to be defined. The benefits realization plan must be monitored regularly to track the progress of each of the key milestones identified for each benefit profile.

Benefit Evaluation

This should take place at a prescribed time or can be event-driven such as stage gates or when there is an important project event or milestone. It is carried out to ensure that benefits realization is still on track and if not, immediate changes should be made to the benefits realization plan. Benefit evaluation should be carried out for benefits still to be realized and those that have been realized. For realized benefits, it will generate information regarding what has been achieved. The objectives of benefits reviews are to update the benefit realization plan to ascertain that the identifield benefits are still achievable; inform relevant stakeholders of the progress made toward realizing the benefits; assess the performance of the new or improved operations against their original baseline performance levels; and assess the level of benefit achieved against the benefit realization plan.

CHAPTER 12

The Ingredients of an Effective Project Control Environment

Introduction

The final chapter of this book is devoted to the embedding and promotion of an enabling environment for effective project control. As evident from previous chapters, one of the underlying principles of the PCIM project control methodology is that project control does not operate in a vacuum as it is affected by many factors in the organizational environment (see Chapters 4 and 5 for a detailed discussion on this). In essence, it is not enough for an organization to just have the right processes and tools for project controls; an organization also requires an environment that enables them. This means putting in place the ingredients that support effective project controls dedicatedly. Organizations need to develop deliberately well-designed and intelligent project controls. Figure 12.1 depicts the ingredients that are essential components of such a well-designed and intelligent project control process.

These ingredients are discussed in the sections to follow.

Simplicity and Ease of Use (Simplify Project Controls)

Project control processes, procedures, and systems should be simple, clear, and easy to implement. Poorly designed controls can be overly time consuming and demanding of data, leading to a perception of it outweighing any benefit. Although implementation of project control is a relatively straightforward process, poorly designed project controls can become too complicated for its users. Design of controls needs to be done intelligently and proportionately, ensuring that there is a balance between the time

Integration of cost and time

Clarity and visibility
of expectations

Simplicity and
ease of use

Project
control
environment

Clearly defined
process

People centric
and training

Collaborative approach

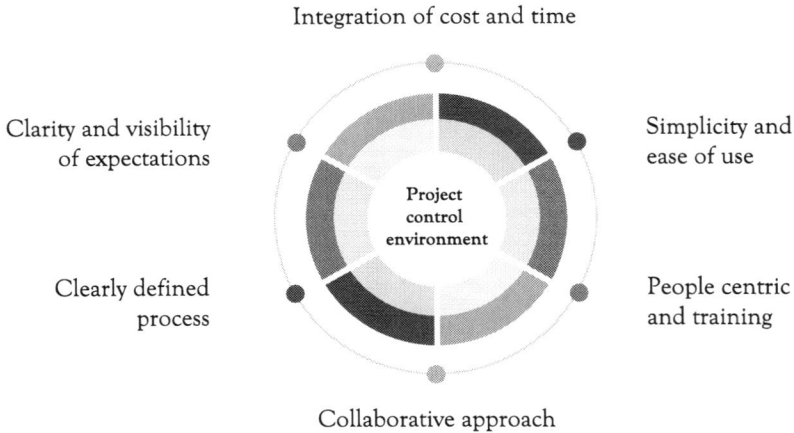

*Figure 12.1 Key ingredients of an effective project control
environment*

spent operating the control and the added value. Effective project control processes get this balance right so that project staff will be willing to adopt, without perceiving it as extra work but instead seen as part of their project management duties.

People-Centric and Training

A project control regime that aspires to be effective should be designed considering the requirements and needs of the people who will be implementing it, especially project delivery and operational staff. Project controls should be aligned to strategic objectives and be designed considering the requirements and needs of the people who will implement them. People are crucial for the smooth operation of any project control process, since any level of analysis and subsequent control will be provided by them. Therefore, project controls would be more effective if project delivery and project management staff understood the science of project control better. However, according to a survey by the PMI (2018), only 45 percent of organizations have a formal process for developing project management competency. An organization that is serious about delivering projects effectively should not only put in place the necessary project control systems and processes but also needs to provide the necessary training needed to implement them correctly.

Collaborative Approach

There is a general tendency to make project control the sole responsibility of a function within an organization such as the project management office, project controls, cost management quantity surveying, commercial, or even finance. For a project control system to be effective, it is important to develop a culture that makes the governance and adherence to project controls not just a matter for a single function but for all areas of an organization. The implementation of effective project controls requires the cooperation of different project stakeholders and coordination among the different departments within an organization, built on a clear understanding of why it is important.

Clearly Defined Processes

Quite often, project controls are too focused on highly configured, complex IT systems, and not focused enough on core processes and practices. Systemization of project control processes is still extremely important; in fact, it is recommended as a key enabler of good project management. However, organizations should not disregard the importance of the processes and practices that will generate the information and data needed to implement the systems. Effective project controls can and should be IT-enabled, but always based on clearly defined core processes.

Clarity and Visibility of Expectations

Have you ever joined an organization and found a process or system difficult to follow? A project control process that will be effective should show adequately what is expected during the various steps of the process. One of the key challenges to effective control of many types of projects is the complexity resulting from the interface, phases, and stages of projects. Project control is also a cycle involving planning, monitoring, reporting, analyzing, and action uitilizing many technical and management processes. Many project controls in practice do not highlight adequately what is expected during the various areas and steps of the control process. For effective project control to be achieved in practice, it is important that lines of communication are clear, and the most up-to-date information is communicated on time and to the relevant persons during the project control process.

An overly prescriptive project control process is not the solution and is not what is being recommended here since projects differ in characteristics. However, project delivery staff on-site, project management leadership, and office-based project staff would find it helpful if project control processes and systems can be easily followed through visibly knowing what is expected, and if possible, the reasons for this during all aspects of the project control process. The project control approach to be adopted on a project needs to be planned at the outset of a project so that the project management team is aligned. Due to the varied level of experience of the project team members, alignment on project control approach is only achievable with the setting up of an organizationwide project controls guidelines and procedures to be utilized for projects in the organization.

Integration of Cost and Time

The interrelationship existing between cost and time during project controls cannot be overstated. For example, as has been discussed previously in this book, the research that informed the PCIM project control methodology revealed that the leading factors inhibiting effective cost control and time control of capital projects are similar (see Chapter 5). But despite this, organizations often don't integrate cost and time controls in practice as revealed by the PCIM project control research (see Chapter 3). For project control to be effective, organizations must integrate cost and time from the start including at the core of the design of their project control process.

Conclusion

To conclude, this book has argued that project controls tools and techniques do not in themselves make up the project control process because project control is so much more than them. For example, project controls consist of practices that are deployed during the implementation of the project control process. Nondeployment of good practices for the various aspects of the project control process will be detrimental to the project control effort. These practices represent the "how" of project control and differentiate the effectiveness of the project control effort from one project to another or from one organization to another. In addition to practices, it has been shown that the maturity of the project control environment of an organization is also key to the effectiveness of project controls. This book has identified three key categories of "environmental" issues that affect the effectiveness of project controls. Two of these categories (challenges of project controls in practice—see Chapter 3 and project control inhibitors—see Chapter 5) are negative issues in the project control environment that need to be understood, prevented, and mitigated, while the third category of issues as discussed in this chapter are a collection of positive factors (ingredients of an enabling project control environment). In essence, this book and the PCIM project control methodology have shown that the organizational climate in which projects are undertaken has a relationship with project outcomes. Organization's cultural attributes such as transparency and openness will enable project issues to be raised more freely so they can be dealt with before becoming even bigger problems. Additionally, organizations that have continuous improvement, coaching, mentorship, and role modeling as part of its culture will develop competent project control professionals consistently. Positive outcomes from cultural factors like these underscores the importance of creating an enabling environment for project controls, which will lead to more successful delivery of projects by organizations.

References

Anantatmula, V., and P. Rad. 2018. "Role of Organizational Project Management Maturity Factors on Project Success." *Engineering Management Journal* 30, no. 3, pp. 165–178. DOI: 10.1080/10429247.2018.1458208

Artto, K., T. Ahola, and V. Vartiainen. 2016. "From the Front End of Projects to the Back End of Operations: Managing Projects for Value Creation Throughout the System Lifecycle." *International Journal of Project Management* 34, no. 2, pp. 258–270.

Association for Project Management (APM) 2010. "Introduction to Project Control." Princess Risborough: APM.

Association for Project Management (APM) 2015. "Planning, Scheduling, Monitoring and Control: The Practical Project Management of Time, Cost and Risk." Princess Risborough: APM.

Association for Project Management (APM) 2019. "APM Body of Knowledge." (APM BoK), Princes Risborough: APM.

Ballesteros-Péreza, P., K. Elamrousy, and C. González-Cruzc. 2019. "Non-linear Time-cost trade-off Models of Activity Crashing: Application to Construction Scheduling and Project Compression with Fast-tracking." *Automation in Construction* 97, pp. 229–240.

Bryde, D., C. Unterhitzenberger, and R. Jober. 2018. "Conditions of Success for Earned Value Analysis in Projects." *International Journal of Project Management* 36, pp. 474–484.

Camilleri, E. 2016. "Project Success: Critical Factors and Behaviours." London: Routledge, pp. 12–14. Available online https://doi.org/10.4324/9781315602493 (accessed March 01, 2022).

Chalmers, J., and M. Armour. 2019. "The Delphi Technique." In *Handbook of Research Methods in Health Social Sciences*, ed. P. Liamputtong. Singapore: Springer.

Chan, P., D. Ho, and C. Tam. 2001. "Design and Build Project Success: Multivariate Analysis." *Journal of Construction Engineering and Management* 127, no. 2, pp. 93–100.

Chang, A. 2002. "Reasons for Cost and Schedule Increase for Engineering Design Projects." *Journal of Management in Engineering* 18, no. 1, pp. 29–36.

Davis, K. 2014. "Different Stakeholder Groups and Their Perceptions of Project Success." *International Journal of Project Management* 32, pp. 189–201.

Egan, J. 1998. "Rethinking Construction: The Report of the Construction Task Force." London: Department of Trade and Industry.

Fewings, P., and C. Henjewele. 2019. *Construction Project Management: An Integrated Approach (third edition)*. London: Routledge.

Flostrand, A., L. Pitt, and S. Bridson. 2020. "The Delphi Technique in Forecasting—A 42-Year Bibliographic Analysis (1975–2017)." *Technological Forecasting and Social Change* 150, p. 119773.

Flyvbjerg, B. 2017. "Introduction: The Iron Law of Megaproject Management Chapter 1." *The Oxford Handbook of Megaproject Management*, pp. 1–18. Oxford: Oxford University Press.

Flyvbjerg, B., M. Holm, and S. Buhl. 2003. "How Common and How Large are Cost Overruns in Transport Infrastructure Projects?" *Transport Reviews* 23, no. 1, pp. 71–88.

Harris, F., R. McCaffer, and F. Edum-Fotwe. 2013. "Modern Construction Management (seventh edition)." Oxford: Blackwell-Wiley.

Irfan, M., S. Khan, N. Hassan, M. Hassan, M. Habib, S. Khan, and H. Khan. 2021. *Role of Project Planning and Project Manager Competencies on Public Sector Project Success Sustainability* 13, no. 3, p. 1421. https://doi.org/10.3390/su13031421

Jergeas, G., and J. Ruwanpura. 2010. "Why Cost and Schedule Overruns on Mega Oil Sands Projects?" *Practice Periodical on Structural Design and Construction* 15, no. 1, pp. 40–43.

Jung Y., and S. Woo. 2004. "Flexible Work Breakdown Structure for Integrated Cost and Schedule Control." *Journal of Construction Engineering and Management* 130, no. 5, pp. 616–625.

Kanwala, N., M. Zafarb, and S. Bashira. 2017. "The Combined Effects of Managerial Control, Resource Commitment, and Top Management Support on the Successful Delivery of Information Systems Projects." *International Journal of Project Management* 35, no. 8, pp. 1459–1465.

Kezner, H. 2017. "Project Management: A Systems Approach to Planning, Scheduling, and Controlling (12th edition)." Hobeken: Wiley.

KPMG. 2019. "Independent Review of CrossRail—Financial and Commercial." *KPMG.* https://content.tfl.gov.uk/financial-and-commercial-redacted.pdf (accessed March 01, 2022).

Larson, E. 1995. "Project partnering: Results of study of 280 construction projects." *Journal of Management in Engineering* 11, no. 2, pp. 30–35.

Lester, A. 2017. "Project Management, Planning and Control: Managing Engineering, Construction and Manufacturing Projects to PMI, APM and BSI Standards (7th edition)." Oxford: Butterworth-Heinemann.

Lock, D. 2013. "Project Management (10th Edition)." London: Routledge Taylor and Francis Group.

Luo, L., Q. He, J. Xie, D. Yang, and G. Wu. 2017. "Investigating the Relationship between Project Complexity and Success in Complex Construction Projects." *Journal of Management in Engineering* 33, no. 2, p. 04016036.

Meredith, J., S. Shafer, and S. Mantel, Jr.. 2021. "Project Management: A Managerial Approach (11th edition)." Chichester: Wiley.

Munizaga, N., and Y. Olawale. 2022 (In Press). "Leading Factors and Root Causes of Delay and Cost Overrun of IT and construction Projects in the Retail Industry in Chile." *International Journal of Project Organisation and Management.*

National Audit Office. 2013. "Over-Optimism in Government Projects." Report by the National Audit Office. www.nao.org.uk/wp-content/uploads/2013/12/10320-001-Over-optimism-in-government-projects.pdf (accessed March 01, 2022).

Nicholas, J. 2020. "Project Management for Engineering, Business and Technology." London: Routledge.

O'Neil, C. 2019. "Global Construction Success." Chichester: John Wiley and Sons Ltd.

Oh, J., H. Lee, and H. Zo. 2021. "The Effect of Leadership and Teamwork on ISD Project Success." *Journal of Computer Information Systems* 61, no. 1, pp. 87–97.

Pollack, J., and D. Adler, 2016. "Skills That Improve Profitability: The Relationship Between Project Management, IT Skills and Small to Medium Enterprise Profitability." *International Journal of Project Management* 34, no. 5, pp. 831–838.

Project Management Institute. 2018 "Pulse of the Profession 2020." Newtown Square: Project Management Institute. www.pmi.org/-/media/pmi/documents/public/pdf/learning/thought-leadership/pulse/pulse-of-the-profession-2018.pdf (accessed June 03, 2022).

Project Management Institute. 2020. "Pulse of the Profession 2020." Newtown Square: Project Management Institute. www.pmi.org/-/media/pmi/documents/public/pdf/learning/thought-leadership/pulse/pulse-all-comparison-reports-final.pdf?v=dd7afb39-1fe0-4063-923f-11410463244d (accessed March 01, 2022).

Project Management Institute. 2021. "Project Management Body of Knowledge (PMBoK) (Seventh edition)." Newtown Square: Project Management Institute.

Reuters. 2022. "London's $24 Billion Crossrail Finally Opens." www.reuters.com/world/uk/londons-24-billion-crossrail-finally-opens-2022-05-23/ (accessed June 07, 2022).

Rezvani, A., A. Changa, A. Wiewioraa, N. Ashkanasy, P.J. Jordan, and R. Zolina. 2016. "Manager Emotional Intelligence and Project Success: The Mediating Role of Job Satisfaction and Trust." *International Journal of Project Management* 34, no. 7, pp. 1112–1122.

Sanchez O., M. Terlizzi, and H. Moraes. 2017. "Cost and Time Project Management Success Factors for Information Systems Development Projects." *International Journal of Project Management* 35, 8, pp. 1608–1626.

Seymour, T., and S. Hussein. 2014. "The History of Project Management." *International Journal of Management and Information Systems* 18, no. 4, pp. 233–240.

Shariff, N. 2015. "Utilising the Delphi Survey Approach: A Review." *Journal of Nursing Care* 4, no. 3, pp. 246–251. http://ecommons.aku.edu/eastafrica_fhs_sonam/38 (accessed March 01, 2022).

Shenhar, A., D. Dvir, O. Lever, and A. Maltz. 2001. "Project Success: A Multidimensional Strategic Concept." *Long Range Planning* 34, no. 6. pp. 699–725.

Snow, A., M. Keil, and L. Wallace. 2007. "The Effects of Optimistic and Pessimistic Biasing on Software Project Status Reporting." *Information and Management* 44, no. 2. pp. 130–141.

Sourani, A., and M. Sohail. 2015. "The Delphi Method: Review and Use in Construction Management Research." *International Journal of Construction Education and Research* 11, no. 1, pp. 54–76.

Tokdemir, O., H. Erol, and I. Dikmen. 2019. "Delay Risk Assessment of Repetitive Construction Projects Using Line-of-Balance Scheduling and Monte Carlo Simulation." *Journal of Construction Management and Engineering* 145, no. 2, p. 04018132.

Turner, J. 2006. "Towards a Theory of Project Management: The Functions of Project Management." *International Journal of Project Management* 24, no. 3, pp. 187–189.

Vandevoorde, S., and M. Vanhoucke. 2005. "A Comparison of Different Project Duration Forecasting Methods Using Earned Value Metrics." *International Journal of Project Management* 24, no. 4, pp. 289–302.

Young, R., and S. Poon. 2013. "Top Management Support—Almost Always Necessary and Sometimes Sufficient for Success: Findings From a Fuzzy Set Analysis." *International Journal of Project Management* 31, pp. 94–957.

Zaman, U., L. Florez-Perez, M.G. Khwaja, S. Abbasi, and M.G. Qureshi. 2021. "Exploring the Critical Nexus between Authoritarian Leadership, Project Team Member's Silence and Multi-dimensional Success in a State-owned Mega Construction Project." *International Journal of Project Management* 39, no. 8, pp. 873–886.

Zwikael, O., and J. Meredith. 2021. "Evaluating the Success of a Project and the Performance of its Leaders." *IEEE Transactions on Engineering Management* 68, no. 6, pp. 1745–1757.

About the Author

Dr. Yakubu Olawale is Associate Director, Major Projects Advisory at KPMG UK where he consults, advises clients, provides assurance, and strategic insights for boards, government, and leaders of organizations in relation to their capital projects, programs, and infrastructure investments. He is also a board member at Pioneer Group and a member of its finance, audit, and assurance committee. He has more than 20 years of experience in the areas of project control, project management, commercial management, and project consultancy across many sectors including construction, IT, telecom, financial services, infrastructure, pharmaceutical, facilities management, government, and energy. Prior to joining KPMG UK, he held senior positions at FTSE 100 and 250 companies in the UK and was also a lecturer at Aston University. He is qualified in multiple areas including as a project manager, chartered accountant (ACMA, CGMA), chartered surveyor (Fellow of the Royal Institution of Chartered Surveyors) (projects, cost, and contracts), chartered construction manager (MCIOB), and a fellow of the Higher Education Academy (FHEA). He holds a bachelor's degree and further completed an MSc in Environmental Engineering and Project Management at the University of Leeds, a PhD at the University of the West of England, Bristol, and an MBA at the University of Warwick. He is passionate about effective project controls and his research works have been published in leading academic journals including *International Journal of Project Management, Construction Management and Economics Journal, Journal of Management in Engineering*, and the *International Journal of Project Organization and Management*.

Index

Acceptance risk response strategy, 187–188
Actual cost, 148, 157, 158
Actual cost of work performed (ACWP), 157, 158
Adequate planning, 47, 57, 93
Analyzing, for project control, 102, 113–116
Arrow diagram method (ADM), 123
Association for Project Management (APM), 2, 22, 29, 146, 171, 173
Association for Project Management Book of Knowledge (APM BoK), 166, 169
Authorization gate, 49–50
Avoidance risk response strategy, 186

Bar charts, 126–129
Benefits management, 200–202
Book of Knowledge (BoK), 22
Budget at completion (BAC), 159
Budgeted cost of work performed (BCWP), 157, 158
Budgeted cost of work scheduled (BCWS), 157, 158
Business case process, 198–200

Change impact analysis, 171
Client representatives, 51–52
Communication problems, 51
Contracts
    adversarial forms of, 50–51
    noncollaborative forms of, 50–51
    schedule, 37
Cost breakdown structure (CBS), 106, 107, 114, 116
Cost control, 24, 162–163
    cost value reconciliation (CVR), 150–154
    inhibitors, 78–82

overview, 145–146
profit and loss system, 146–147
program evaluation review technique (PERT), 148–150
S-Curve, 154–161
standard costing, 148
suitability, appraisal of, 161–164
unit costing, 147–148
Cost performance index (CPI), 43, 158, 159, 161
Cost value reconciliation (CVR), 9, 116, 150–151
    advantages, 152–153
    cost reconciliation, 151–152
    good practices, 153
    limitations, 154
    value reconciliation, 152
Cost variance (CV), 158
CPI. See Cost performance index (CPI)
Critical path method (CPM), 9, 105, 108, 110, 133–136, 142
CVR. See Cost value reconciliation (CVR)
Cybernetic control, 25
Cyclic project control
    planning, 101, 104–108
    monitoring, 101–102, 108–111
    reporting, 102, 109, 112–113
    analyzing, 102, 113–116
    Delphi process, 102–104

Decision tree, 182–183
Delphi process, 102–104
Disciplinary/organizational function approach, 177

Earned value, 157
Earned value analysis (EVA), 42, 43, 46, 65, 71, 105, 116, 156–161

measures, 157–159
advantages, 159–160
disadvantages, 160–161
Earned value management (EVM), 9, 156–161
Environment, social, and governance (ESG), 194
Estimate at completion (EAC), 159

Fallback risk response strategy, 187
Feedback control, 25–26
Feed-forward control system, 26–27
Financial wastage, 2

Gantt charts. *See* Bar charts
Go/no-go controls, 25
Graphical evaluation and review technique (GERT), 124, 139–141, 143, 144

Inhibitors, 76–77
Investment appraisal, 200

Key performance indicators (KPIs), 97, 98, 100, 192–197

Line of balance (LOB) method, 129–132, 142
Loss system, 146–147

Master schedule, 37, 122
Milestone date programming, 124–126, 142
Monitoring, 32, 101–102, 108–111
Monte Carlo simulation, 184

Network-based schedules, 124
Nonfactual reporting, 55–56
Non-network-based schedules, 124

Organizational cultural change, 70–71
Organizational inhibitors, 77–78

PDM. *See* Precedence diagram method (PDM)

Performance evaluation and review technique (PERT), 9, 136, 140, 141, 143, 149–150
advantages, 138
disadvantages, 138–139
time estimation, 136–138
Performance indicators (PIs), 192–193
Performance standards, 27–28
PEST/PESTLE, 176–177
Planned value (PV), 157, 158, 161
Planning, 28–31, 101, 104–108
Postcontrol, 25
Precedence diagram method (PDM), 124, 132–133, 139, 141, 143, 144
Predetermined approach, by organization, 177
Product breakdown structure (PBS), 169
Profit system, 146–147
Program evaluation and review technique (PERT)
cost control techniques, 148–150
time control techniques, 136–139, 143
Progressive elaboration, 178
Project-based inhibitors, 78
Project contractors, 90, 96
Project control, 57
action, 39–40
analysis, 39
challenges, 43–44
from client, 44, 49–52
from organization, 44–46
from project delivery approach, 44, 47–49
from project team, 52–56
concept, 22–23
cost
estimation, 40–41
monitoring, 41
reporting, 42
performance analysis, 42–43
action, 43
cycle, 27–34
duration assessment
tasks and activities, 36–37
visual representation, 37–38

environment
    collaborative approach, 205
    cost and time, 206
    key ingredients, 203–204
    people-centric and training, 204
factors, 23–27
inhibitors, 68
overview, 1–3, 21–22
in practice, 35
process, 3–4
monitoring and reporting, 38–39
types, 25–27
Project control implementation
        document (PCID), 62, 63, 73
Project control inhibitors
        management (PCIM), 8, 15,
        35
    action, 66–67
    analysis, 64–65
    for effective project control, 10–11
    execution phase, 62
    exogenous inhibitors, 76–77
    endogenous organizational
        inhibitors, 77–78
    endogenous project-based
        inhibitors, 78
    feedback, 65–66
    framework, 11
    good practice measures
        corrective good practice
            measures, 83
        design and scope changes, 84–85
        organizational good practice
            measures, 83–84
        preventive good practice
            measures, 82–83
        for risks and uncertainties,
            85–98
    implemention, barriers to, 70–72
    methodology, 60–68
    monitoring, 63
    planning, 61–62
    project control inhibitors, 68
    project control methodology
        case study, 72–74
        checklist, 68–69
        research process, 12
        scalability, 69–70
    reporting, 63–64

revise plan, 67
Project cost accounting system
        (PCAS), 149
Project execution plan (PEP), 31, 93
Project investment success (PIS), 6
Project management success (PMS), 6
Project master schedule, 37
Project ownership success (POS), 6
Project scope management, 22, 24,
        166
    components, 166–171
    overview, 165
    work breakdown structure (WBS),
        171–173
Project success measurement
        approach, 7

Quantitative cost risk analysis
        (QCRA), 89, 185
Quantitative risk analysis techniques,
        89, 181
    costing risk, 183
    decision tree, 182–183
    Monte Carlo simulation, 184
    quantitative cost risk analysis
        (QCRA), 185
    quantitative schedule risk analysis
        (QSRA), 184–185
    sensitivity analysis, 181–182
    three-point estimating/probabilistic
        method, 184
Quantity surveyor, 40, 42, 63, 150

Reduction risk response strategy, 186
Relative importance index (RII),
        78–80
Reporting, 32, 102
Revise plan, 67
Risk drivers, 179
Risk management
    overview, 175–176
    systematic approach
        risk analysis, 180–185
        risk classification, 176–178
        risk identification, 178–180
        risk response, 185–189
Risk matrix, 180
Risk register, 88, 179–180

Schedule at completion (SAC), 159
Schedule performance index (SPI),
    43, 158
Schedules, 37–38, 90, 122. *See also*
    Time control
Schedule variance (SV), 158
Scope creep, 165
S-curve, 154–161
Senior management, 45–46
Sensitivity analysis, 181–182, 200
Sharing risk response strategy,
    188–189
SPORT, 177
Stage schedule, 37
Standard costing, 148
Subcontractors, 93, 95–99
Supplier performance management
    evaluation approach, 193–194
    information collection, 194
    key performance indicators (KPIs),
        192–193
    overview, 191–192
    performance data analysis, 194–195
    performance indicators (PIs), 192
    reporting, 195–196
    review and feedback, 196–197
Supply chain management, 96

Target schedule, 37
Tender schedule, 37
Three-point estimating/probabilistic
    method, 184

Time control, 24, 162–163
    critical path method (CPM),
        133–136, 142
    graphical analysis, 126–129, 142
    graphical evaluation and review
        technique (GERT), 139–140,
        141, 143
    inhibitors, 78–82
    line of balance (LOB) method,
        129–132, 142
    milestone date programming,
        124–126, 142
    overview, 121–124
    precedence diagramming method
        (PDM), 132–133, 143
    program evaluation and review
        technique (PERT), 136–139,
        143
Transfer risk response strategy, 187

Unit costing, 147–148

Variance at completion (VAC), 158,
    159

WBS. *See* Work breakdown structure
    (WBS)
"What-if" analysis, 182
Work breakdown structure (WBS),
    16, 106, 107, 116, 122, 169,
    171–173

OTHER TITLES IN THE PORTFOLIO AND PROJECT MANAGEMENT COLLECTION

Timothy J. Kloppenborg, Xavier University and
Kam Jugdev, Athabasca University, Editors

- *Managing Projects With PMBOK 7* by James Marion and Tracey Richardson
- *Shields Up* by Gregory J. Skulmoski
- *Greatness in Construction History* by Sherif Hashem
- *Inner Building Blocks* by Abhishek Rai
- *Project Profitability* by Reginald Tomas Lee
- *Lean Knowledge Management* by Forsgren Roger
- *Moving the Needle With Lean OKRs* by Bart den Haak
- *The MBA Distilled for Project & Program Professionals* by Clark Brad
- *Project Management for Banks* by Dan Bonner
- *Successfully Achieving Strategy Through Effective Portfolio Management* by Frank R. Parth
- *Be Agile Do Agile* by Vittal Anantatmula and Timothy J. Kloppenborg
- *Project-Led Strategic Management* by James Marion, John Lewis, and Tracey Richardson
- *Hybrid Project Management* by Mark Tolbert and Susan Parente
- *Design: A Business Case* by Brigitte Borja de Mozota and Steinar Valade-Amland

Concise and Applied Business Books

The Collection listed above is one of 30 business subject collections that Business Expert Press has grown to make BEP a premiere publisher of print and digital books. Our concise and applied books are for...

- Professionals and Practitioners
- Faculty who adopt our books for courses
- Librarians who know that BEP's Digital Libraries are a unique way to offer students ebooks to download, not restricted with any digital rights management
- Executive Training Course Leaders
- Business Seminar Organizers

Business Expert Press books are for anyone who needs to dig deeper on business ideas, goals, and solutions to everyday problems. Whether one print book, one ebook, or buying a digital library of 110 ebooks, we remain the affordable and smart way to be business smart. For more information, please visit www.businessexpertpress.com, or contact sales@businessexpertpress.com.

Printed in Great Britain
by Amazon